Natural History Society of Queensland

Transactions of the Natural History Society of Queensland

Natural History Society of Queensland

Transactions of the Natural History Society of Queensland

ISBN/EAN: 9783337149703

Printed in Europe, USA, Canada, Australia, Japan

Cover: Foto ©Andreas Hilbeck / pixelio.de

More available books at **www.hansebooks.com**

TRANSACTIONS

OF THE

NATURAL HISTORY SOCIETY

OF

QUEENSLAND.

VOL. I.

1892-3-4.

Brisban
PRINTED BY POLE, OUTRIDGE & CO., PETRIE'S BIGHT.
MDCCCXCV.

THE NATURAL HISTORY SOCIETY OF QUEENSLAND.

This Society was established at a meeting held in Brisbane on the 14th January, 1892.

OBJECTS:

1. The cultivation of a taste for Natural History.
2. The investigation of the physical features—geology, fauna, flora, etc.—of the surrounding country.
3. The dissemination of the knowledge acquired.

OFFICERS AND COUNCIL:
1892.

President : HENRY TRYON.
Vice-President : T. P. LUCAS, M.R.C.S.
Hon. Secretary and Treasurer : F. WHITTERON.

Council :

R. ILLIDGE.	H. G. STOKES, F.G.S.	A. J. TURNER, M.D
J. LAUTERER, M.D.		C. J. WILD, F.L.S.

1893

President : HENRY TRYON.
Vice-President : A. JEFFERIS TURNER, M.D.
Hon. Secretary and Treasurer : R. ILLIDGE.

Council :

T. P. LUCAS, M.R.C.S., &c.	H. G. STOKES, F.G.S.	A. J. TURNER.
R. H. RELTON.		F. WHITTERON.

1894.

President : T. P. LUCAS, M.R.C.S., &c.
Vice-President : C. J. WILD, F.L.S.
Hon. Secretary and Treasurer : R. ILLIDGE.

Council :

G. GROSS.	R. H. RELTON.	H. TRYON
A. T. O. PRESTON.		F. WHITTERON.

CONTENTS.

iv.

TRANSACTIONS.

The Natural History Society of Queensland.

THE GENUS *ANTHERÆA* AS ILLUSTRATING FACTS OPPOSING DARWINISM.

BY

Thomas P. Lucas, M.R.C.S.E., L.S.A. Lon., &c., &c.

(Read on 3rd March, 1892).

THE WHISTLING MOTH.

BY

Henry Tryon.

(Read on 7th April, 1892).

The habit of producing sound is met with in but few kinds of lepidopterous insects, and quite rarely is this sound of the nature of stridulation. And this being so the fact that a small, but select, series of Buderim Mountain insects brought last year to the Queensland Museum by Mr. W. Riebe, contained—as their donor pointed out—a sound-producing moth, was not without interest. This insect was afterwards recognised by the writer as being Hecatesia fenestrata, Boisduval (Fam. Zygænidæ), from acquaintance with the figures of this and the allied species H. thyridion, Feisthamel, in Appendix F. (by Adam White) to Sir George Grey's "Journals of Two Expeditions of Discovery in North-west and West Australia." It would appear that even prior to 1841, the date of publication of this work,

the special noise emitted by Hecatesia fenestrata had been noticed, and the special mechanism connected with its production pointed out; although this fact has escaped the notice of more recent writers on entomological subjects, not excepting Hagen, until that keen observer, the late Henry Edwards, visited Australia in 1889, and afterwards recorded, in " Insect Life," vol. ii., his personal observations. The remarks H. Edwards makes are of such interest that no apology is needed for their being incorporated in this note. He writes concerning H. fenestrata :— " During my residence in Australia I was collecting insects in the Plenty Ranges, about twenty miles from Melbourne, and in the burning heat of midday sun had sat down to rest and pin my captures under the shade of a thick acacia tree. I was astonished, and almost startled, at a peculiar sound apparently very near me, which was unlike anything I had ever heard, and which I at first thought was the voice of some unfamiliar bird. I listened attentively, looking in the direction of the noise, but could see nothing. I took up my net and walked up the opening in the woods, the sound still continuing, and greatly exciting my curiosity. It was very loud and distinct, and not unlike ' Whiz whiz ' repeated by the mouth with the teeth closed. I had proceeded about thirty yards when the noise suddenly stopped. I sat down and waited, thinking I should again hear it and be able to trace it to its source. I was not disappointed, for in a few minutes it again appeared, and this time quite close to me. I looked very carefully, and in an opening, buzzing about with a swaying lateral motion, were two or three insects, which at first sight I took to be some species of Hymenoptera. I gave a sweep with my net and made a capture, which was soon within my collecting bottle. My heart beat violently, as I found that I had taken a lovely black and orange moth such as I had never before seen. The structure by which the insect is enabled to produce the singular and striking sound is the thickening of the costal membrane about the apical third, behind which and nearer to the centre of the wing is a rather broad vitreous space extending almost to the median nerve, this space being transversely ribbed, as are the bundles of eggs in some species of orthoptera. The antennæ are thickened at the tips into a sort of prolonged club, pointed at the extreme end, and with the

under side of the terminal joints horny and devoid of cilia.
These striking as they would do in flight at the will of the
insect against the transverse ribs of the transparent space cause
the whizzing and characteristic sound that so attracted me, and
which is doubtless intended as a call of love to the individual of
the weaker sex, who sits enthroned in the branches listening
with delight to the noisy homage of her many lovers." In conclusion, what appears likely to prove a new species of Hecatesia
was recently brought under my notice by Mr. R. Grieve. In
November, 1891, Mr and Mrs. Grieve repeatedly both heard and
saw generally in the early morning what they describe as a
" whistling moth." This was in dry level timbered country,
the prevailing trees being Casuarina and Scribbly Gum, at Broad-
water, near Brisbane. Concerning this moth, my informants
relate that " it had a quick and jerky flight, and that individual
examples, though perhaps not in every instance, gave forth
during flight a sibilant legato whistle. The solitary example
secured by Mr. Grieve formed the object of a pencil sketch by
him. It proves to be a female, and is remarkable for having but
one white transverse band on the forewings; the large orange
spot on the hind wings is, too, without the usual excavations.
Strange to relate, as H. Edwards has pointed out, the geographical distribution of the species of this genus is peculiar. Of the
five recorded species four are Australian and one inhabits
Mexico.

Note.—Mr. R. Illidge, at a meeting of the Society, held on
5th May, 1892, exhibited specimens of a small brown noctuid
named Beressa natalis, Walker, remarking that though a common insect the habit to which he was about to allude did not
appear to have been previously recorded. The moth was a
small brown insect with a wing expansion of nearly eight-
tenths of an inch, and the male had a small round tympanum-like
clear depression in the middle of the forewing. Sound was
produced, by the male only, whilst it was in flight, and though
slight was distinctly audible. The insect whilst emitting it was
observed to keep up a hovering motion over or around one spot
where probably its consort was at rest.

NOTES ON GRACILLARIA

BY

A. JEFFERIS TURNER, M.D., LOND.

(Read on 5th May, 1892).

[*Note.*—The substance of this memoir (*vide* "*Queenslander,*" 14th May, 1892) amplified with descriptions of several new species, was communicated subsequently to the Royal Society of South Australia (*vide* "*Trans. Roy. Soc. of South Australia,*" vol. xviii, pp. 120-138, 1894.—ED.]

--- --- --- ---

THE BEAN MAGGOT.

BY

HENRY TRYON.

(Read on 5th May, 1892).

THE living insects before you are small, black, two-winged flies which are provisionally named Oscinis phaseoli. My attention was first directed to this insect from having reared it some four years since from bean plants, the victims of a diseased condition, received from Bulimba. Since then evidence has come to hand that it is especially injurious to leguminous vegetables, not only about Brisbane, but also in the Sherwood, Tingalpa, and other districts ; in fact it bids fair to minimise the yield of such desirable plants as the French beans, and possibly also of the horse grams. As a typical instance of its depredations, a case reported by Mr. J. W. A. Campbell, a gardener to Sir S. W. Griffith, may be cited. This observer states that the Negro beans, the Belle Don or butter beans, the Governor Denison beans, and Chinese bean (Dolichos sp.), have been affected by this pest at New Farm during the last four years, and recently more prominently so ; and that successive crops—from December onwards—have been completely destroyed by it.

The injury under notice is occasioned by the fly whilst the latter is in the maggot condition, but the plant supports the insect during every phase of its existence, its transformations being undergone within its tissues. Beans affected by this redoubtable pest present the following features :—The plants affected—and the injury may be evinced when they are less than a fortnight old—fail to make the amount of growth which they do when in a healthy state. They are altogether stunted, and oftentimes break off level with the ground. They may also flower, but if any pods are borne these are few in number, are very much twisted, swollen in different parts, and do not exhibit the usual crispness in fracture. From the point where the roots originate to where the plant emerges from the ground there is almost complete decay, and immediately above this the stem is irregularly swollen, becoming less so in passing upwards to the extremity of the branches. The epidermis covering the swollen part is generally fissured, especially near the ground, and these fissures in favourable seasons may emit adventitious roots, which, however, seldom reach the soil. It is also light-brown or brownish white in colour, and separable, presenting the appearance of being injured through instant contact with some blistering or corrosive liquid. If the plant has been for some time subjected to the attacks of the bean-maggot all its branches, and even the peduncles of its flowers as well as its leaf stalks, are similarly injured, each part presenting, however, to a certain extent, special features. The branches, besides being thickened, are usually shortened, and more or less contorted, so also are the leaf stalks, and both may break off through being decayed at their point of insertion. On removing a portion of the epidermis in any part affected the pest will be brought to light, maggots of small dimensions—or their pupæ—being everywhere met with.

The maggot is a translucent, yellowish, elongate, cylindrical, twelve-jointed grub, obtuse at each extremity, and rather broader towards the head; it measures $1\frac{1}{4}$ to $1\frac{1}{2}$ lines in length.

The puparium is a parallel-sided object rounded at each end and about 1 line in length. If the injury is of long continuance it will be observed, in exploring the plant from the base upwards, that the empty pupa cases, the pupæ, and the maggots are successively met with.   Nearly a hundred individuals in different stages of growth may be detected in a single bean-plant, though but 10in. or less in extreme height.

The fly, which is quite a small though conspicuous insect, with its wings directed obliquely backwards, is black, but its eyes present beautiful copper-coloured and green reflections, and its wings have an opalescent glimmer when viewed in certain positions.   It deposits its eggs in the first instance upon or within the tissue of the bean plant when the latter is still quite young, perhaps even before the first true leaves have expanded ; and the injury is then inflicted in the stem immediately above the surface of the ground, the maggots feeding both upwards and downwards, just beneath the epidermis.   Having attained their full dimensions they pupate *in situ;* and the flies as they emerge deposit their eggs higher upon the plant at the insertion of a stem leaf or flower-stalk, the maggots of the second generation still feeding upwards, just beneath the skin.   The pest is assisted in its progress through the plant-tissue by a large and stout hook-shaped toothed apparatus in front of the mouth, and by rows of sharp papilla just behind the head, and at the joints separating each body segment.   As a rule the maggots are not met with within the central hollow of the stem itself, except when they can gain access to it, for pupating, either at the dead portion at the " collar " of the plant, or where a decayed spot occurs through the falling-off of a branch.   The pupæ, however, generally occur, as do the maggots, just beneath the epidermis. The maggot attains its full size within a few days, and the fly emerges from its chrysalis (puparium) after the lapse of ten days —or less, if the weather is warm.

The technical description of the pest in its different phases is postponed, but the symptoms of its presence and the facts of its life history are enlarged upon, since it is by these that its presence may be recognised, and so steps be taken for its extirpation.   Probably it will everywhere prove equally destructive at first to dwarf French beans, and to these especially, with a possible tendency to attack the horse gram.   It has been suggested that this Oscinis, as being partial to leguminous plants, will devastate the lucerne paddocks, but there is some reason to think that this will not be the case. It is more than probable that it is a native insect, although the attempt to detect its presence in indigenous Leguminosæ has hitherto failed. How far it approaches in character the American Oscinis trifolii, also a small, rather robust, black fly, cannot at present be ascertained, since F. M. Webster, formerly of La Fayette, who first discovered it in 1886, has not yet published a sufficiently detailed description.

The diet of the pest being restricted, it is recommended that whenever the presence of the latter is detected the entire growing crop should be destroyed, and the ground occupied by it planted for a time with other vegetables. By this means it is hoped that the Oscinis may be locally stamped out. It is, however, interesting to record that at present it is preyed upon by two different kinds of minute hymenopterous insects. These are exhibited under the microscope, and there are also on view the living insect and its parasites, as well as drawings illustrating the ovipositor of the female fly, and the mouth-hook, and curious pedunculated spiracles of the maggot.

[Mr. R. ILLIDGE, during the discussion which this paper elicited, informed the meeting that he had met with the bean-maggot in his garden at Bulimba, and believed he had got rid of it by adopting a procedure similar to that recommended.—ED.]

CHALCEDONY.

BY

HENRY G. STOKES, F.G.S.

(Read on 5th May, 1892 : *vide* " *Queenslander*," 14th May, 1892).

THE PARASITE OF THE FRUIT MAGGOT.

BY

HENRY TRYON.

(Read on 5th May, 1892).

THE fruit maggot of Queensland—the larval form of a small wasp-like fly, a species of Tephritis—is one of the worst pests which the orchardist has to contend with in any part of the world. It is probable that at present it is responsible for the destruction of considerably more than half of the fruit grown in the southern part of the colony, excluding the consideration of bananas, grapes, and perhaps oranges, which fruits it does not attack to any large extent. We may meet with it plentifully in our apples, pears, quinces, peaches, nectarines, apricots, plums, guavas, Brazilian cherries, pomogranates, and to a less extent in persimmons and the citraceous fruits. Such an extended notice of it has already been given in my " Insect and Fungus Pests " (*vide* pp. 54-74) that no occasion exists for further dealing with it this evening, except to mention one fact—namely, that it is now being kept in check by an insect which is parasitic upon it. Living examples of the adult Tephritis and its parasite are before you.

During my investigation into the life history of the fruit maggot it more than once happened that small hymenopterous insects belonging to the family Braconidæ were observed wending their way with peculiar characteristic flight—not rapid, but jerky, with quick and continuous vibration of the wings—amongst the boughs of trees the fruit of which had been observed to be " maggotty " and above such of the crop as had fallen to the ground. Ever and anon the tiny insect would alight on a fruit as if to explore it. However, until quite recently the fact of its parasitism on the fruit maggot, which was early suspected, could not be placed beyond dispute. A few months since Mr. J. W. Strachan, in the course of a series of experiments undertaken for the purpose of testing the operation of a new insecticidal agent, had occasion to rear some fruit flies from Brazilian cherries infested by fruit maggots, and some small hymenopterous insects having hatched out together with the insects sought, Mr. Strachan consulted me with a view to learn whether they had arisen from the fruit as vegetable feeders or whether they were parasitic upon the maggots. Having seen similar insects previously under the circumstances above mentioned, and knowing the habits of the Braconidæ, I inclined to the latter opinion. Quite recently, while temporarily residing in the Tingalpa district, I met with the hymenopteron as before, but in much larger numbers, about a fruit-laden guava-tree, and I decided thereupon to finally settle the question of its parasitism. With this object in view a number of the puparia and some maggots of the fruit fly were exhumed from the soil beneath the guava tree, and these having been kept under suitable conditions, but without the presence of any foreign material, gave birth to the mature forms of the pest, and amongst them specimens of the parasite, such as you behold in its living state. The latter, as already remarked, is a member of the Braconidæ, and probably a species of Ópius. It is a yellow glossy insect, with conspicuous black eyes. It measures about two lines in length, and has the wings, which expand to five lines, faint smoke-coloured, with pink reflections in certain lights. The antennæ are longer than the body and dark-coloured. The male is rather smaller than the female, which has a short black ovipositor. In repose the wings are placed backwards over the body, and the antennæ directed outwards from it, either forwards or backwards. In countries in which economic entomology is regarded with the attention which is justly due to it, such a parasite as this would be artificially propagated, and so cared for that the ill-effects due to the operation of so baneful an insect pest as is the fruit fly would be considerably lessened.

MIMICRY AND PROTECTIVE RESEMBLANCE.

BY

H. LAMBERT THOMPSON.

(Read on 5th May, 1892 : *vide* "*Queenslander,*" 14th May, 1892).

NOTES ON SOME INSECTS WHOSE FOOD-PLANT IS THE MORETON BAY FIG (*FICUS MACROPHYLLA*).

BY

R. ILLIDGE.

(Read on 11th June, 1892).

[Owing to an emergency the manuscript of this paper was lost from the possession of its author and cannot therefore be reproduced.]

PLANTS OBSERVED DURING A VISIT TO STRADBROKE ISLAND.

BY

C. J. WILD, F.L.S.

(Read on 11th June, 1892).

A SINGLE afternoon's work in midwinter (May) does not, it would seem, promise much worthy of remark ; however, specimens of 150 flowering plants were secured.   Fortunately in examining these I have had the co-operation of our president, Mr. H. Tryon, who, as some of you are aware, examined the flora of the locality during a visit in August, 1882.   The large swamp immediately to the south of the settlement in the first instance engaged my attention.   On the borders of this was found the pink-flowered rutaceous, Boronia ledifolia, and more or less included within its borders the leguminous shrub Aotus lanigera, with its branches densely covered with linear leaves and with sub-terminal large axillary yellow flowers.   Also two shrubs belonging to the same natural order, Leguminosæ—namely, Pultenæa myrtoides, with its orange flowers in dense terminal heads, and Bossiæa heterophylla—a flat-stemmed plant with few leaves, solitary yellow flowers and large flattened stipitate seed pod.   Myrtaceous plants were represented here by the paper-bark tea-tree, Melaleuca leucodendron, which was in full flower, much to the joy of numerous parrots, leather-heads, and other honey-eating birds ; the crimson bottle-brush Callistemon lanceolatus ; Myrtus tenuifolia ; Agonis scortechiniana ; the purple-flowered Melastoma malabathricum ;

Epacris microphylla, with somewhat fastigate branches, cordate
acuminate leaves, and terminal bunches of white axillary flowers ;
the broad-leaved Banksia (B. latifolia). The following amongst
other herbaceous plants were also found in this situation,
namely :—Andrastœa salicifolia (not, however, in flower) ; three
of those interesting insectivorous plants, the Sundews—namely,
Drosera burmanni, with its rosette of radical spathulate leaves ;
D. binata, with its divided or twice dichotomous leaves, and D.
peltata, with its numerous orbicular stem-leaves. An example
of these insectivorous plants, which capture their living food
material by means of small utricles (bladders)—namely, the
Utriculariæ (Fam. Lentibularicæ), was also met with growing in
the mud—merely a slender hair-like erect stem, with a few purple
flowers, probably U. uliginosa. There was also obtained here
the white-flowered fragile Mitrasacme indica ; Stylidium debile,
with its mechanically irritable flower column ; Lobelia anceps ;
the amaryllid Hæmodorum tenuifolium ; Xyris operculata, with
its yellow flower forming a terminal head ; Commelyna cyanea ;
Eriocaulon, with grass-like leaves and white flowers compacted
into a rounded knob. In the same swamp were also gathered
examples of numerous species of rushes (Juncaceæ), Cyperaceæ,
including the handsome Cyperus lucidus and Restiaceæ including
Restio tetraphyllus with its curious contorted foliage. The
swamp-loving grasses were represented by Paspalum distichum,
Leersia hexandra, with its six stamens ; Ischæmum muticum,
and others. Club-mosses by Lycopodium laterale or a close
ally, and Selaginella uliginosa. Finally, amongst ferns were
Gleichenia dicarpa, Lindsæa dimorpha, a large Aspidium, seeming
to be equally related to both A. molle and A. unitum and
Blechnum serrulatum.

At the foot of the hills running north and south, with an
aspect towards Moreton Bay, were secured Hibbertia linearis,
Elæocarpus cyaneus, a handsome shrub with conspicuous cobalt-
blue somewhat large fruits ; Zieria lævigata ; the so-called native
hop plant—Dodonæa triquetra ; the leguminous bush Gompho-
lobium virgatum, with trifoliate leaves and conspicuous somewhat
large yellow flowers, also a second species (G. pinnatum) of the
same genus, not in flower ; Acacia juniperina, a low shrub with
acicular foliage ; the native raspberry, Rubus parvifolius ; the

myrtaceous plants Leptospermum microphyllum, with its copious
foliage of tiny leaves and conspicuous though small white
flowers; Leptospermum stellatum; the epacrids Leucopogon
lanceolatus, L. leptospermoides, and L. ericoides—the first
mentioned a most superb shrub, its whole outer surface covered
with little spikes of white blossoms, lending it a most effective
appearance.   Here also were two species of Persoonia—namely,
P. cornifolia and P. linearis—both with yellow flowers, but the
former with broad lanceolate leaves, whilst the latter had linear
ones.   In addition to these two Proteaceæ was a third species
of the same order, Lomatia silaifolia, a low shrub with thrice
pinnate light green leaves and large racemes of wax-like white
flowers.   This plant, which is one of the choicest of our wild
flowers, might with other Stradbroke Island plants worthily
find a place in our gardens; preserved in the Hortus Siccus of
the botanist its inflorescence unfortunately assumes a black
colouration; no lover of flowers can, however, having once seen
it growing, forget its most handsome appearance.   To proceed,
here again were met with Pimelea linifolia and Wikstrœmia
indica; also the handsome euphorbiaceous shrub with its white
flowers and bright green linear leaves, Ricinocarpus pinifolius.
There were also two plants in which the true leaves were almost
absent or represented by very diminutive organs of this kind—
namely, the euphorbiad Ampera spartioides and Choretrum
candollei (Fam. Santalaceæ).   Ascending the wood-clad hills,
there was little undergrowth in the sandy soil, but here and
there on the flanks and on the summit were bushes of the
yellow flowered leguminous shrub, Dillwynia ericifolia, and in
the latter situation Conospermum taxifolium, a linear, small
leaved proteaceous plant, bearing at other seasons dense spikes of
white flowers.   Two species of Loranthus occur parasitically
upon the trees.   Of the latter many different kinds were noticed,
though botanical specimens of all were not secured.   The island
in fact is well wooded, although the trees are usually of small
growth.   Hibiscus tiliaceus, Vitex trifoliata, the usual
mangroves of temperate Australia, and others grow near the sea
shore, and away from it are met with two species at least, of
eucalyptus, two honeysuckles—Banksia æmula and B.
integrifolia, Exocarpus cupressiformis, the oak—Casuarina

suberosa, and the Cyprus pine—Callitris robusta; and in
addition to these are the previously-mentioned tea trees—
Melaleuca leucodendron and Callistemon—both affecting damp
low-lying spots. Amongst herbaceous plants growing away
from the swamps specimens were secured of the blue-flowered
Ionidium, I. filiforme, the leguminous climbers Hardenbergia
monophylla and Glycine tabacina; Trachymene procumbens,
Calotis cuneifolia, Helichrysum bracteatum, and H. apiculatum,
Velleia spathulata, the strange-looking fern Schizæa dichotoma.
On the immediate seaboard were found the large convolvulus,
Convolvulus pes-capræ, the legume Canavallia obtusifolia, and
the blue-flowered lobelia, Dampiera stricta. Amongst naturalised plants, or indigenous species growing as weeds, the following
were collected—namely, Malvastrum tricuspidatum, Sida
rhombifolia, Geranium, sp. (scented variety), Oxalis corniculata,
or sour grass; Gnaphalium luteo-album, Bidens pilosa, or
"cobblers' pegs" (Bailey); Galinsoga parviflora, the annual
mercury; Tagetes glandulifera, the stinking Rodgers; Vittandia,
sp.; Sonchus oleraceus, sow thistle; Wahlenbergia gracilis, the
Australian harebell; Asclepias curassavica, the cotton weed;
Solanum nigrum, the night-shade; Verbena bonariensis;
Lantana camara; Chenopodium ambrosioides, the Mexican tea;
Euphorbia pilulifera, the asthma spurge; Ricinus communis,
the castor oil plant. Time would not admit of the pasturage
being critically examined; the abundance of the introduced
buffalo grass in the paddocks was, however, remarked, also the
presence of Paspalum indicum and Cynodon dactylon, both
predominant species.

BIRDS OBSERVED DURING A VISIT TO STRADBROKE ISLAND.

BY

H. CONNAH.

(Read on 2nd June, 1892).

[*Note.*—This paper related to the birds—but few in number
and variety—met with by the author on the occasion of an
excursion on the part of the Society made in May, 1892: *vide*
" *Queenslander,*" 11th June, 1892.—ED.]

PROGRESSIVE MODIFICATIONS OF AMBULATORY LEGS IN ANIMALS INTO OTHER ORGANS.

BY

JOSEPH LAUTERER, M.D.

(Read on 16th June, 1892).

[*Note.*—The substance of this paper was communicated on 8th April, 1893, to the Royal Society of Queensland: *vide* " *Proc. Roy. Soc. Qld.*," vol. x, pp. 19-20.—ED.]

ALUMINIUM AND THE CLEVELAND KAOLIN.

BY

HENRY G. STOKES, F.G.S.

(Read on 7th July, 1892).

SEVERAL letters having of late appeared in the daily papers bearing on the discovery of a supposed valuable clay in the Cleveland district, termed by some of the writers thereof alumina, and by others kaolin, containing aluminium ; and as apparently a good deal of misunderstanding appears to exist concerning the importance or otherwise of this discovery the accompanying facts are submitted in the hope that they may serve to remove it.

Now, this difference of opinion to which allusion is made relates to the value of the so-called kaolin as a source of the earth alumina and so of the metal aluminium ; also on its value as a china clay.

It is convenient at the outset to consider what alumina is. This mineral, then, is an oxide of the element aluminium, and is in fact the only oxide of that metal known. In nature it occurs in two states or conditions—(1), *free,* when it may (*a*) be anhydrous or (*b*) contain water of constitution ; and (2) in a *combined state.* As illustrations of the former of these modes of occurrence we have the mineral corundum and its varieties— ruby, sapphire, &c.—which is an anhydrous oxide ; whilst as the best-known instance of the hydrated oxide we have the so-called mineral bauxite. As examples again of alumina in a combined state we have the mineral spinel, of which again there are several varieties, which is the oxide of aluminium combined with the oxide of magnesium; and kryolite, the fluoride of aluminium and sodium. By far the best illustration of this last mode of occurrence is, however, the hydrous silicate of alumina-clay, which enters so largely into the composition of clayey-slates, shales, and earths, and of this the Cleveland mineral is an example. The hydrous silicate of alumina, or clay, when occurring in an approximately pure condition, is termed kaolin; usually, however, it exists in a more or less impure state, the impurity consisting of sand, carbonate of lime, oxides of iron, and the alkalies; whilst in many cases more or less carbonaceous matter is present.

Passing in review these different combinations under which alumina is met with, as possible sources of the metal aluminium, we may at once eliminate the clays and kaolins, since it has nowhere been found practicable to utilise hydrous silicate of alumina for its manufacture, owing to the great difficulty and consequent expense of liberating the alumina from the silica with which it is chemically combined. Incidentally, too, it may be here pointed out that in published analyses of clays giving alumina as occurring in a certain percentage, this should be regarded as being chemically combined with more or less of the silica which is represented in the same tabulation, since as above stated alumina does not exist in a free state in them. Again we may pass over the different gems illustrating the occurrence of alumina, either free or combined, already mentioned. In short, aluminium is at present derived from two sources only—namely, the above-mentioned minerals, kryolite and bauxite, neither of which, as far as can be ascertained, are yet known to occur in these colonies.

In the case of the former of these, i.e., kryolite, the double fluoride of aluminium and sodium, which was until quite recently extensively employed as a source of aluminium, it may be pointed out that the impurities which it contains (principally iron and silicon compounds), and a limited supply, have of late years detracted from its successful use. This mineral occurs most extensively at Evigtock, in West Greenland, and is shipped in quantity to Europe and the United States, where it is used for making aluminium, soda, soda and alumina salts, and—in Pennsylvania—for the manfacture of a white glass resembling porcelain in appearance. In April of the present year the powdered kryolite was quoted in the market at £20 per ton for small quantities, a price which would of course be much reduced for parcels in bulk of unassorted mineral (*vide* " *Engineering and Mining Journal.*")

Bauxite—a name derived from Beaux, near Arles, in France, where large deposits of the mineral occur—is then the substance whence aluminium is now principally derived. In addition to the above-mentioned locality in France it is now known that there are vast deposits of it in Ireland, and that it also exists in considerable quantities in the States of the American Union—North Carolina and Georgia. The grey shale, quoted by John D. Hennessy in the *Courier*, 27th June, 1892, as being sold on the Continent of Europe at £2 17s. per ton, is probably the popular name in commercial circles for bauxite. It contains no less than from 60 to 80 per cent. of its weight of alumina, almost the whole of which is free when its water of constitution is not taken into consideration. The following is the average composition of the mineral as shown by chemical analysis :—Alumina, 64·24 ; silica, 6·29 ; oxide of iron, 2·40 ; lime, 0·55 ; magnesia, 0·88 ; soda, 0·20 ; potash, 0·46 ; water, 25·74 ; total, 100·26.

In the manufacture of aluminium from bauxite, the alumina is first separated chemically from iron, silica, and other impurities. It is then washed, dried, and calcined at a red heat for a considerable time. There are several methods available for treating the alumina for aluminium. The Pittsburg Reducing Company reduce the metal from the prepared oxide (alumina) by electrolysis, the aluminium being held in solution by a molten fluoride bath, which is itself not decomposed by the electric current.

The Cleveland deposits being, as we have seen, of no value as sources for either alumina or aluminium, it remains to consider whether they correspond in character to the best descriptions of clays such as kaolin or china-clay, premising that in so much as there is a superabundance of clay suitable for both pottery and bricks in the immediate neighbourhood of Brisbane, the discovery of additional deposits of this class is of little or no commercial interest.

In estimating the suitability of a clay for the manufacture of china, the following factors have to be regarded:—First, as to its composition, what quantity of silicate of alumina does it contain, and to what extent are impurities associated with this silicate? Secondly, the nature of the treatment required to eliminate these impurities? Thirdly, the amount of clay of uniform quality available? For these are the questions which have to determine its employment as a commercial success or otherwise.

In the case of what is known under the different names of kaolin, china clay, porcelain clay, or Cornish clay, we have a hydrous silicate of alumina with certain impurities, which when the latter are removed has the following average percentage composition, namely:—Silica, 47·2; alumina, 31·1; and water, 18·7; that is, regarding the silica as wholly combined a clay containing 67·93 per cent. of silicate of alumina, and 11 per cent. of free silica. The abovementioned impurities, which comprise small quantities of lime, iron, alkalies, and (quartz) sand, are almost entirely removable by a simple process to which the clay is submitted before being placed on the market or converted into chinaware. In fact it is found that the preparation of the clay for the market involves an expenditure of only 17s. per ton and that it is sold at prices ranging up to 35s. per ton.

The Cleveland clay, in the light of the Aldershot analysis, quoted in the correspondence to which allusion has already been made, contains by analysis 56·60 per cent. of silica and 33·02 per cent. of alumina, that is, regarding again the alumina as wholly combined, 71·4 per cent of silicate of alumina and 18·22 per cent of free silica. Judging from samples which have come to hand the Cleveland clay also lacks uniformity in its physical characters, such as colour, texture, &c., a condition of things indicative of a variability also in chemical composition. In fact

c

it seems more nearly to resemble a pottery than it does a china
clay.

Pottery clay, as is well known, varies exceedingly in composition both in the amount of silicate of alumina and in that of
free silica and other impurities which it contains.   Analysis
showing samples to yield from 44 to 58 per cent of silica, 23 to
24 per cent of alumina, 1 to 7 per cent of oxide of iron, and 10
to 15 per cent of water.

[*Note.*—As a result of the false importance assigned to these
clay beds, applications had even been made to the authorities
for prospecting areas ; the community is therefore indebted to
the author for dispelling the illusions which had arisen regarding
them.—Ed.]

SILVER AND ITS OCCURRENCE IN NATURE AS ILLUS-
TRATED BY THE RIVERTREE ORES.

BY

Edgar Hall, F.C.S.

(Read on 4th August, 1892: *vide "Queenslander,"* 20th August, 1892).

A NEW TOBACCO PEST.

BY

HENRY TRYON.

(Read on 4th August, 1892).

WHEN in 1889 attention was drawn by me to those diseases —due to the attacks of insects—which affect our potatoes, the existence of a formidable pest in our midst—the caterpillar of a small moth named Lita solanella—was for the first time brought under notice. In my " Report on Insect and Fungus Pests " (pages 175 to 181) this insect, as it appears in the different phases of its existence, is fully described, and its habits as well as the nature and extent of its ravages are dwelt upon. It is there stated that this potato grub was reported as occurring in Tasmania as early as 1855, though still prior to this it had manifested its presence in New Zealand. Soon after 1870 it was noticed in one locality in New South Wales as doing considerable damage to potatoes grown there, and by 1881—or earlier still—it had displayed its destructive propensities in South Australia. In the meanwhile, however, it had found its way to Algeria, in 1874, proving very injurious to the potatoes in that remote locality. In 1889 an extensive literary research had failed to reveal any mention of the existence of this pest either in America or on the continent of Europe. However, with regard to the former region Albert Koebele, of the Entomo- logical Branch of the United States Agricultural Department, during a recent visit informed me that by aid of the description of the pest in the above report he had been able to identify it with a potato enemy which he had recently detected as occurring in California amongst shipments of this esculent. When it first appeared in this colony cannot, perhaps, now be ascertained. Concerning the extent of the ravages which it occasions it may be mentioned that Boisduval, in writing of its occurrence in Algiers, remarks that during a single season three-fourths of the potato crop was destroyed by this pest, and Otto Tepper, when in 1881 alluding to his Adelaide experiences, states that as far as his continued observations went, the insect was causing in its caterpillar or grub condition the destruction of hundreds of tons of potatoes every year, and that during late years he had scarcely been able to get half-a-dozen pounds without finding a considerable percentage more or less affected by it. But it is not necessary to go beyond the colony of Queensland for evidence of the immense loss which the potato grub occasions. In the early part of the present year the potatoes which arrived from the Southern markets were to a large extent worm-eaten or already rotten, as every housewife must needs have observed—and here also, the pest was in evidence. As already pointed out by me, this formidable pest is not only conveyed from place to place in the tuber itself, but is also transmitted whilst still adherent to the sacks or other receptacles which have contained affected potatoes.

At first its attention here was confined to the contents of the storeroom, and even as late as 1889 no instance of its attacking the growing crop in Queensland had come under my notice, though it was suspected to be enacting this rôle ; but it had been already ascertained that wherever it occurred here it soon visited such of the tubers as had been unearthed. However, in December of the following year—1890—on visiting a cultivation in the district of Moggill, near Brisbane, a patch of still growing plants was found to be affected by the presence of the pest, and, in fact, was in rapid process of destruction. An important trait in the habit of the insect which has not been remarked by any previous writer was observed on the occasion of this visit. It being noticed that the larva of the moth was not confining its attention to the tubers but was also mining in the tissue of the leaves, on which it occasioned a brown spotted appearance. This interesting feature in the habits of Lita solanella was not, however, observed with surprise, since an example of the perfect insect had been previously reared by me in a potato leaf forwarded from Toowoomba. The chief interest, however, in this communication resides in what is to follow.

Insects are better judges of botanical affinities between plants than are, in many instances, ourselves. The cabbage worm, Plutella cruciferarum, which we know too well, recognises

the close relationship which exists between the plant from which
it derives its name, and the wild mustard, and is equally partial
to both ; the caterpillars of our commoner species of Papilio
similarly recognise the fact that the Chinese box-leafed Atalanta,
the introduced orange and its allies, and the native species of
Citrus, though to our observation so different in appearance,
have close affinities—as pronounced by botanists who have
placed them in the same rutaceous tribe, Aurantiæ—and are
found feeding upon all these plants. In the case of Lita solanella,
the pest under consideration, it has been observed by me that it
has now become inimical to the growth of the tobacco plant as
well as to that of the potato, both—so unlike in their habit—
being members of the same natural order, Solanaceæ. Shortly
after the visit to the growing potatoes already alluded to advice
was sought as to the best method for contending with a pest
which defied repeated efforts to raise to maturity tobacco in the
same Moggill district ; and the damaged young plants submitted,
in illustration of the nature of the ravages of the assailant com-
plained of, were found to have their leaves extensively mined by
tiny caterpillars, which—by use of the breeding cage—were demonstrated to be those of the potato grub. It was also found
that caterpillars reared from eggs laid by the same generation of
moths so obtained, fed indifferently upon the potato and tobacco.
Having made this discovery, and in view of the commercial relations which obtain between Brisbane and the remote districts
(" worm-eaten " potatoes having been seen by me on their arrival
at a small centre of population where also potatoes are grown,
thirty-five miles distant by dray road from Dalby, and in the
same month of December), the transmission of this pest to the
well-known tobacco-growing district of Texas, and its establish-
ment there was not altogether an unexpected event. And such
event was brought to my notice in November, 1891, when advice
was sought as to the best method for contending with the in-
cursion of an interesting Peronospora* which had been discovered
by me in 1889 as the cause of an also formidable disease of the
young tobacco plant now known as " blue mould." Amongst
the leaves forwarded from Texas on this occasion, and exhibiting

* *Vide* leaflet issued by Department of Agriculture entitled "Tobacco
Disease," 19th June, 1890.

this plant parasite, there were two mined—as in the case of the Moggill plants—by the caterpillar of the potato grub. These were bright green with large pale brown, translucent, sharply-defined patches, bounded by curved lines. Near one edge of the leaf, which was infolded, tiny black particles of "frass" were observable. Feeding in the tissue intervening between the two surfaces of the leaves themselves were the tiny caterpillars—one in each leaf.

Whether the caterpillar of Lita solanella will thrive also on other solanaceous plants than the potato and the tobacco—to which it has been shown to be so partial—has not yet been ascertained. If, however, the common "blackberry" of our colonial youth—the nightshade, Solanum nigrum—will support it, so generally distributed is this weed of cultivation that the chances of persistence of the pest in any district are by no means small. When once it is in a cultivation it is doubtful whether it will be found practicable to effectively employ any deterrents to ward off its attacks. Feeding as it does beneath the surface of the tobacco leaf, and thus protected, the application of any of the usual insecticides when once it has manifested its presence will prove futile. Generations of the insects also quickly succeed one another. It behoves every one, therefore, who would stay its attacks to destroy at once all plants affected, that its propagation may be checked. If not too late in the day it is also recommended that no potato be introduced from outside to a tobacco-growing district. Certainly not potatoes which in their tissues harbour the pest.

RANATRA AND ITS HABITS.

BY

R. H. RELTON.

(Read on 18th August, 1892 : *vide* "*Science Gossip*," 1879, for a paper on subject whereof that under above title was a transcript).

INSECT PESTS IN THE STORE.

BY

HENRY TRYON;

(Read on 18th August, 1892 : *vide* "*Queenslander,*" 27th August, 1892).

[*Note.*—This paper related to Anobium paniceum, Sitophilus oryzæ, Gnathocerus cornuta, Tenebrioides mauritanicus, &c., found feeding upon Rice paper.—ED.]

CRYPTOLÆMUS MONTROUZIERI, OR THE SCALE INSECTS' ENEMY.

BY

HENRY TRYON.

(Read on 1st September, 1892).

THE trunks of the handsome bunya trees growing along the river banks of our Botanical Gardens are at present conspicuously marked by snow-white spots and blotches. On examination this will be found to be due to the presence of small active six-footed grubs, resembling what all horticulturists recognise as "mealy bugs," measuring about ¼in. in length, and covered above with six rows of contiguous opaque white mealy appendages, which being of the nature of secreted matter are easily removable. Clusters of those grubs, in crannies in the bark, in a quiescent condition, will also be encountered, and amongst them some similarly clothed pupæ. Creeping slowly amongst the scales of the trunk surface will also be noticed small oval beetles, measuring about ⅛in. in length and ⅛in. in breadth, having the head, the corselet, the extremity of the wing covers, and the under surface in part, red; whilst the greater portion of the wing covers above and the thorax beneath is black. The whole surface is also finely punctured, and thickly clothed with close greyish pubescence. Transferring our observations to the foliage of the bunya, it will be noticed that these snow-white grubs and the less conspicuous beetles, are wandering amongst it also; and further examination will reveal the fact that their attention is being occupied by a species of coccus—or cochineal insect—with which the trees are badly infested. This coccus (named Dactylopius auricariæ) will be recognised on the under surfaces of the leaves as presenting the appearance of small grains of sulphur, for so it appears in its early condition of life. And on the stems themselves, often heaped together in vast numbers, will be found small tumid black bodies with a raised yellow central dorsal stripe, a similarly coloured one on either side, and a massive mauve-coloured heap at one extremity. These bodies, which are examples of the adult coccus, are easily injured, and then stain any body which may come in contact with them a decided purple. The mauve-coloured heap referred to is the ovisac and its contents. In fact the relationship which subsists between the beetle and the white grub on the one hand and the Dactylopius auricariæ on the other, is that of a carnivorous insect and its prey. The discovery of this interesting connection was published by me in July, 1889, in my report on "Insect and Fungus Pests" (page 16), when dealing with the discrimination between friends and foes amongst insects, being made known in these words:—"It is, however, for destroying our scale insects that the Coccinellidæ (ladybirds) are here most highly useful. To mention but a single instance, that of a small black beetle reddened at each extremity, belonging to the group Scymnites and named Cryptolæmus. The larva of this is a small active grub, measuring ⅓in. in length, covered above with six rows of contiguous, elongated, white mealy, secreted appendages. Quite recently the bunya bunyas and other auricaraceous trees growing about Brisbane have been infested by a coccus insect—an apparently undescribed species of Dactylopius, which affects especially the spot where the leaves and branches unite ; and these parasites were at one time so numerous that the death of these valuable trees from their attacks seemed very imminent. However, the Cryptolæmus beetle also visited the Auricarias, and in some places its larvæ occurred in such profusion that the trunks of these trees, and the ground around their bases, looked as if flour had been dusted in patches here and there upon them. Both in its adult and larval condition it waged war upon the coccid insects, and as a result these trees are saved from destruction. This friendly insect is none other than the one which is met with on various native trees, especially acacias, and also on the citraceous and other economic plants of our gardens. These also it visits for the purpose of ridding them, or at least checking the increase, of the various scale insects, especially those belonging to the Lecanidœ which infest the trees, and these pests it literally mows down to the surface of the leaf, so great being its voracity. That such an obvious fact should have escaped observation, much less comment, seems scarcely credible, and yet it is so. Further than this, wherever the writer has been, either at Toowoomba or Brisbane, the larva of this insect has been regarded as the mealy bug (another coccid unhappily becoming now too prevalent about Brisbane), and, under a mistaken idea, destroyed by those who make a practice of killing destructive insect-visitants to their crops." The same insect is again alluded to on page 185 of the same report.

The importance of this discovery to the agricultural interest, though lost sight of here, has been fully recognised in other countries, as may be concluded from the remarks which are to follow. The Hon. Ellwood Cooper, President of the State Board of Agriculture of California, in the course of his opening address to the Thirteenth State Fruit-growers' Convention, after quoting largely from my report on insect and fungus pests as far as it related to "parasites and predaceous insects," and reading, amongst other extracts from it, the one cited concerning Cryptolæmus, concluded, " I will not copy further, but the numerous parasites and predaceous insects described in the work ought to impress upon our minds the importance of an immediate investigation, even if only a semblance of fact should be credited to the report. I urge, therefore, that we memorialise Congress for an adequate appropriation to defray the necessary expenses of a specialist to go to Australia and adjacent islands to investigate these reported predaceous insects." We next learn that the Californian State Legislature, as a result of such memorial, appropriated $5000 for sending some one to Australia for the purpose of searching for beneficial insects, and placed this sum at the disposal of the United States Government, which in turn transferred it to the State Department of Agriculture with a view to effecting the object desired. Accordingly, Albert Koebele, an officer in the Entomological Branch of the department, whose

special aptitude for the work had already been abundantly
displayed, left America for Australia in August, 1891. In the
course of the travels which his mission involved, Mr. Koebele
twice visited this part of the colony, and procured in addition to
other insects, the utility of which had already been made known
by me, numerous examples also of the insect with which this
note is especially concerned. And it is gratifying to learn, by
latest advices from Washington, that Mr. Koebele's visit has been
so far successful, that living examples of Cryptolæmus montrouzieri have been transferred from Australia to America for the
behoof of fruit-growers there. In conclusion the early history of
this insect may be here alluded to, as it also is not without
interest. The beetle, then, was first collected in Australia by
the celebrated naturalist-missionary, Pierre Montrouzier in the
"Fifties," and shortly afterwards described by Mulsant in the
3rd volume of his " Opusules Entomologiques " (p. 140), under
the name which it now bears—namely, Cryptolæmus, from two
Greek words signifying hidden scythe, in allusion to the fact that
the mouth organs are concealed by the projecting breast-plate,
and Montrouzieri as commemorative of its discoverer. However
it does not appear that either Montrouzier noted, or Mulsant
suspected, the important rôle which it enacted as a destroyer of
insect pests. Also until my rediscovery of it in 1889 the fact of
the actual or reputed existence of this beetle in Australia seems
to have escaped the notice of students of Australian coleoptera.
Though this useful beetle is in its larval condition such a
conspicuous object, being noticeable at a distance of several
yards, it never seems to be itself consumed by insectivorous
birds. It is not remakable therefore that it should have imitators
amongst insects which do not, it is thought, possess this immu-
nity. These comprise two apparently undescribed beetles—(1)
a Cryptocephalus, and (2) a Rhizobius. In the first of these the
similitude resides in colour and size only, in the latter both
livery and form are repeated. The specimens illustrating this
statement, were in one instance obtained with Cryptolæmus on
a single wattle tree, and were thought at first to be identical
with it.

CRYPTANDRA LONGISTAMINEA.

BY

C. JULIAN GWYTHER.

(Read on 20th October, 1892).

[THIS paper related to the characters of a pretty heath-like rhamnaceous plant having white tubular flowers, described in the " Flora Australiensis " (vol. i., pp. 443), and more recently by the Colonial Botanist (Botany Bulletin, No. 4). The plant had been found flowering during the months of August and September on the Maryvale Run, in the parish of Gladfield—Warwick, where it occurred upon the dry elevated ridges of the range amongst basaltic rocks, growing to a maximum height of three feet, being densely shrubby, and forming circular masses, extending from two to three feet, with occasional much longer offsets. The banks of the Condamine River was the only previous habitat from which it had been recorded, and there it had been collected by the late C. H. Hartmann. *Abstract*—ED.] *vide* " *Queenslander*," 29th October, 1892.

THE OCCURRENCE OF THE ESCULENT FUNGUS, *MORCHELLA DELICIOSA*, IN QUEENSLAND.

BY

C. JULIAN GWYTHER.

(Read on 20th October, 1892).

THIS interesting fungus was found on the 18th September, 1892, growing on damp loamy soil amongst the rotting bark of a eucalypt, on the bank of a tributary of Freestone Creek, Warwick, draining the southern slopes of Mount Dumaresq and the adjacent hills, and known as Charley's Gully. A dried specimen forwarded to Mr. F. M. Bailey, Colonial Botanist, was determined by him as being Morchella deliciosa, one of the four species of morells occurring in Victoria, their only, until now, recorded

Australian habitat. There were but half-a-dozen individual
fungi in the cluster noticed, nor could further examples be discovered. The largest specimen examined was about 2in high
with a width of pileus or head of 1¼in. The latter is irregularly
conical and reticulate on the outer surface, being furnished with
different sized cells, which are generally hexagonal in outline.
Those at the summit are small or obsolete, whilst towards the
base of the pileus they enlarge. They are from two to three
lines broad, by from three to five or six lines long (high), and
from two to three lines deep. The colour of the pileus is dark-
slate-grey inside the cells, with the projecting veins of the latter
of a much lighter hue, and these in some individuals are also
slightly granulated, as apparently in process of ejecting the
spores. The pileus thus taken as a whole very much resembles
some old honeycomb or wasp nest. The stalk, or that which is
designated as such, does not separate from the pileus as in
Agarics, but is fused with it so as to form one piece. It is white,
about 1in. long, measuring from the base of the pileus to the
ground, cylindrical, hollow or sulcate, cottony inside, and enlarges
below to a width of about ½-in. The inside of the pileus forms
an oval cell 1in. long and 3in. or more wide, lined with a white
membrane, slightly granulated near the stalk orifice, which latter
forms an opening 1½ lines wide. The whole fungus is of a soft
and fleshy consistence, and has no smell other than that of the
ordinary edible mushroom (Agaricus campestris).

In Hardwick's "Science Gossip" for June, 1866, there is a
good woodcut of Morchella esculenta, which evidently much
resembles our species, but the figure referred to represents this
European morell as being broader and not so conical as it.

The members of the genus MORCHELLA are essentially
ground fungi, never having been found upon trees or wood.
The word Morchella is derived from the German name for the
fungus—morchel—English, "morell." In Europe it is said to
grow more commonly than elsewhere upon land over which a fire
has run ; hence at one time the German peasants had to be
stopped from burning the forest, a procedure they resorted to for
increasing the supply.

The Morell, as is well-known, is one of the most popular of esculent fungi. It may readily be dried by hanging in a current of air; and, as it loses none of its flavour in undergoing this change, it serves well for flavouring soups, &c., when in this condition, especially if fresh morells or other fungi are not available. It also makes excellent. ketchup, and also, when fresh, forms a delicious dish, especially if stuffed prior to cooking with minced white meat. In Cashmere as well as Europe, where the morell also grows in profusion, it is extensively gathered and held in high repute.

NOTES ON THE SPIDER CELÆNA EXCAVATA.

BY

C. JULIAN GWYTHER.

(Read on 17th November, 1892).

XYLORYCTS, OR TIMBER MOTHS.

BY

R. ILLIDGE.

(Read on 15th December, 1892).

THE moths of the family Xyloryctidæ were known to me many years ago, and the curious habits of the larvæ formed the subject of frequent investigations, but not until the present year did I prosecute any active search for them. This season I have been eminently successful, as the exhibit illustrating these remarks will prove. Many of you I have no doubt have noticed the strange webs mixed with dejectamenta, little bits of bark, and woody matter, which serve to hide the entrance to their burrows or tunnels in the stems and branches of young trees. The caterpillars form these tunnels, and so cover them, I believe, to protect themselves from external foes, such as birds (they are certainly not protection against the ichneumonidæ, for these insects destroy them wholesale), for being fat, naked grubs with only a few slight hairs, they no doubt would form a delicious morsel. In support of this latter opinion we have the fact that the aboriginals in former days sought out these larvæ, cut them out of their holes, and ate them on the spot, as we would an oyster.   These caterpillars are all nocturnal in their habits, and, as far as my researches show, only leave their chamber in the stem during nighttime, when they hurriedly bite off a leaf and retire bearing it off with them.   It is a curious sight to watch them dragging off the leaf and entering the hole backwards (which they do with considerable celerity if at all disturbed), raising at the same time the covering which conceals the entrance to their burrow with their hinder extremity, and pulling the leaf after them.   The leaf is now secured with a few silken threads, and the insect feeds on it at its leisure without fear of being snapped up by some outside enemy.   Some of the species, however, do not appear to feed on the leaves, but devour the soft bark round the entrances to their burrows, spinning the web-covering for some distance, and indeed extending it as they exhaust the food supply in the immediate neighbourhood of the hole.   There is one species at present known which makes no burrow or tunnel, but simply spins its covering on the tree stem and feeds on the soft bark underneath, and when changing to the pupa state forms a cocoon of silk and bits of bark and excrementitious matter mixed.   Others again spin long silken galleries amongst the leaves and twigs, whilst many tunnel into the cones and seed-heads of plants and trees.   Mr. Mèyrick states that T. laetiorella resides in a barricaded tunnel in stems of eucalyptus, etc.; whereas I find it to be a bark-feeder and that it spins a cocoon.   I have reared many and have never found them as stated by him, though it is not unlikely that his statement is correct, for I know Xylorycta luteotactella occasionally to reside in a tunnel in stems of Banksia integrifolia, though usually spinning galleries amongst twigs and leaves, and finally forming a cocoon.   The larger and more characteristic species of the family are all, however, tunnel-makers.   As the larvæ grow bigger they extend the tunnel in size, and this seems to form the chief impediment to rearing them from a young state, as the wood dries up when cut off and becomes too hard for their mandibles, hence they either die in the tunnel or leave it. I have several times succeeded in getting them to form a silken chamber along the interior angle of the box in which they have

been placed, and so reared them without affecting the normal
size of the imago. It is therefore necessary for success in securing the perfect insects to obtain their caterpillars when full-fed
or nearly so, or else when they have already passed to the
chrysalis state. They seal themselves in the burrow when about
to change, and some of them do this very artfully. One or two
species spin out a spout-like web of silk and bits of bark mixed,
which looks like a little piece of dead or decaying stick ; another
species spins a web flush with the bark and so exactly like it
that it is almost impossible for it to be distinguished. Others
again simply spin a strong web inside and across the opening
of the tunnel, whilst some content themselves with only
partially closing the hole with a curved piece of brown horn-like
substance, the nature of which is unknown to me, and occasionally the opening is quite unprotected. Just before pupation
takes place the external covering is usually torn away, and a
very careful search is then necessary to secure examples. They
remain in the pupa state for a very variable period, some emerging in a fortnight or three weeks and others after as many
months. As a rule the trees are not seriously damaged by their
burrows, though odd branches become sickly and die. The
large Maroga unipunctana, however, is an exception, for it feeds
on the bark and frequently eats completely round the stem, thus
ringbarking the tree. · Dogwood and wattle trees may often be
found quite dead above from this cause. On the moth emerging
the hole soon commences to close up and no external trace of it
is left after a little time, except perhaps a slight scar which also
in course of time disappears. The abovementioned M. unipunctana is said to be very destructive in Victoria to fruit trees, but I
have not noticed its appearance here in such trees, possibly
because my experience is limited to my own garden. I have,
however, noted a large species amongst leguminous trees in the
Botanic Gardens, one of which, in front of the curator's house,
has been utterly destroyed by them. The pupæ of the species
of Xyloryctidæ are usually cylindrical, conical at the hinder
extremity and rather flattened towards the head, with one
notable exception. In the insect affording it the chrysalis has
a strange bifurcated projection in front, which appears to be for
the purpose of cutting, auger-like, a way through the very thick

and strong web which the larva spins in front of its tunnel before changing to the chrysalis. Though many of the insects are quite common in the larval state, yet the moths are of great rarity and are seldom seen even by experienced entomologists. Securely as they appear to be hidden in these tunnels, yet they have enemies in various ichneumons with long ovipositors, which find them out and deposit their eggs in their bodies, thus fortunately preventing them from becoming too plentiful. The larva of a beetle belonging to the Cleridæ, Natalis sp., also preys upon them, and finally changes to the perfect state in the gallery lately occupied by the caterpillar of the Xyloryct moth.

Protective resemblance has evidently much to do with the explanation of the different colours and patterns displayed by many of the moths. For example the close similarity in colour between Uzucha humeralis and the bark of the spotted gum and between Cryptophaga nubila and that of the teatree is very obvious, and becomes significant when we remember that the trees mentioned are the food plants of these moths. At the same time other Xyloryctidæ, e.g., C. epadelpha, seem to be coloured in a manner specially suitable for rendering them conspicuous.

LIST OF AUSTRALIAN XYLORYCTIDÆ.

COMPILED FROM WRITINGS OF E. MEYRICK, B.A., F.E.S.; O. B. LOWER, F.E.S.; AND DR. T. P. LUCAS.

An asterisk (*) prefixed to a name denotes the occurrence of that insect in the vicinity of Brisbane.

UZUCHA.—1. * humeralis, *Walk.*. 2. hypoxantha, *Lower.*
PILOSTIBES.—3. * stigmatias, *Meyr.* 4. * enchidias, *Meyr.* 5. tects, *Lucas.*
CRYPTOPHAGA.—6. aglaodes, *Lower.* 7. blackburnii, *Lower.* 8. ochroleuca, *Lower.* 9. * nubila, *Lucas.* 10. * intermedia, *Lucas.* 11. * rubescens, *Lewin.* 12. albicosta, *Lewin.* 13. * pultenaeæ, *Lewin.* 14. * irrorata, *Lewin.* 15. * flavolineata, *Walk.* 16. balteata, *Walk.* 17. russata, *Butl.* 18. phaëthontia, *Meyr.* 19. rubra, *Meyr.* 20. * delocentra, *Meyr.* 21. * epadelpha, *Meyr.* 22. lurida, *Meyr.* 23. * ecclesiastis, *Meyr.* 24. leucadelpha, *Meyr.* 25. hierastis, *Meyr.* 26. proleuca, *Meyr.* 27. * sarcinota, *Meyr.* 28. dolerastis, *Meyr.* 29. stochastis, *Meyr.* 30. cephalochra, *Lower.* ‡[31. stenoleuca, *Lower.* 32. platypedimela, *Lower.* 33. monoleuca, *Lower.*]

Maroga.—34. * unipunctana, *Don.* 35. setiotricha, *Meyr.* 36. * mythica, *Meyr.* 37. * undosa, *Lucas.*

Compsotorna.—38. oligarchica, *Meyr.*

Catoryctis.—39. * tricrena, *Meyr.* 40. * eugramma, *Meyr.* 41. * subparallela, *Walk.* 42. * subnexella, *Walk.* 43. * nonolinea, *Lucas.* 44. * mediolinea, *Lucas.* 45. polysticha, *Lower.*

Phthonerodes.—46. scotarcha, *Meyr.* 47. (P. ?) leucomerata, *Lower.*

Crypsicharis.—48. * neocosma, *Meyr.*

Lichenaula.—49. * undulatella, *Walk.* 50. arisema, *Meyr.* 51. calligrapha, *Meyr.* 52. * lichenea, *Meyr.* 53. laniata, *Meyr.* 54. mochlias, *Meyr.* 55. choriodes, *Meyr.* 56. tuberculata, *Meyr.* 57. musica, *Meyr.* 58. lithina, *Meyr.* 59. monosema, *Lower.* 60. selenophora, *Lower.* 61. * oxygona, *Lucas.*

Notosara.—62. nephelotis, *Meyr.*

Clerarcha.—63. agana, *Meyr.* 64. dryinopa, *Meyr.* 65. grammatistis, *Meyr.*

Plectophila.—66. * electella, *Walk.* 67. discalis, *Walk.* 68. placocosma, *Lower.*

Tymbophora.—69. * peltastis, *Meyr.*

Xylorycta.—70. * porphyrinella, *Walk.* 71. * epigramma, *Meyr.* 72. * flavicosta, *Lucas.* 73. leucophanes, *Lower.* 74. chionoptera, *Lower.* 75. * tinctoria, *Lucas.* 76. * stercorata, *Lucas.* 77. ophiogramma, *Meyr.* 78. synaula, *Meyr.* 79. * strigata, *Lewin.* 80. orcotis, *Meyr.* 81. cosmopis, *Meyr.* 82. * argentella, *Walk.* 83. * luteotactella, *Walk.* 84. * spilonota, *Scott.* ‡[85. homoleuca, *Lower.* 86. sigmophora, *Lower.*]

Telechates.—87. * laetiorella, *Walk.* 88. bipunctella, *Walk.* 89. placidella, *Walk.* 90. parabolella, *Walk.* 91. melanula, *Meyr.* 92. calligramma, *Meyr.* 93. micracma, *Meyr.* 94. * heliomacula, *Lower.*

Chalarotona.—95. craspedota, *Meyr.* 96. insincera, *Meyr.* 97. melitoleuca, *Meyr.* 98. melipnoa, *Meyr.* 99. intabescens, *Meyr.*

Scieropepla.—100. oxyptera, *Meyr.* 101. polyxesta, *Meyr.* 102. reversella, *Walk.* 103. typhicola, *Meyr.* 104. rimata, *Meyr.* 105. liophanes, *Meyr.* 106. acrates, *Meyr.* 107. silvicola, *Meyr.* 108. serina, *Meyr.*

Procometis.—109. lipara, *Meyr.* 110. hylonoma, *Meyr.* 111. bisulcata, *Meyr.* 112. monocalama, *Meyr.* 113. genialis, *Meyr.* 114. diplocentra, *Meyr.* 115. (P. ?) orthosema, *Lower.*

Hypertricha.—116. ephelota, *Meyr.*

Phylomictis.—117. maligna, *Meyr.* 118. monochroma, *Lower.*

Agriophara.—119. * confertella, *Walk.* 120. * gravis, *Meyr.* 121. horridula, *Meyr.* 122. capnodes, *Meyr.* 123. atratella, *Walk.* 124. cinderella, *Newm.* 125. * cinerosa, *Ros.* 126. diminuta, *Ros.* 127. axesta, *Meyr.* 128. * fascifera, *Meyr.* 129. leucosta, *Lower.* 130. leptosemela, *Lower.* ‡[131. cremnopis, *Lower.*]

‡[Note.—The species enclosed in brackets appear to have been missed by the author. They are described in the Transactions of the Royal Society of South Australia, Volume XVIII. for 1893-4.—Ed.]

D

LIST OF PLANTS SERVING AS FOOD FOR THE XYLORYCTIDÆ

WITH INDICATIONS OF THE PARTICULAR INSECTS WHICH AFFECT EACH.

Eucalyptus eugenioides, 72; E. corymbosa, 20, 23, 72; E. maculata, 1, 71; Eucalyptus sp., 27, 71, 87. Tristania conferta, 21 ; T. suaveolens, 10. Eugenia myrtifolia, smithii, 13. Exocarpus cupressiformis ?, 70. Melaleuca leuca-dendron, 9. Daphnandra, 37. Jacksonia, 34, 49. Acacia, 11, 34. Casuarina (common), 14, 39, 40, 41, 43. Elæocarpus grandis, 36. Elæocarpus obovatus, 76. Banksia integrifolia, 15, 72, 79, 83, 84. Cassia, Grevillea robusta, and other plants, 34.

FISH LICE.

BY

HENRY TRYON.

(Read on 12th January, 1893).

[*Note.*—This paper, which was illustrated by typical examples of the crustaceans alluded to, dealt with the members of the families Ægidæ and Cymothoidæ met with upon the Queensland coast, and their respective habits and modifications. Some indication was also afforded of the particular kinds of fish whereupon they occurred.—ED.]

PRESIDENTIAL ADDRESS, 1892.

BY

HENRY TRYON.

(Read on 19th January, 1893).

"A REVIEW OF THE WORK OF THE SOCIETY DURING THE FIRST YEAR OF ITS EXISTENCE."

Vide " Report of the Council for 1892 " : Brisbane, 1893).

BOTANISING ON THE SOUTHERN BORDER.

BY

C. Julian Gwyther.

(Read on 16th March, 1893).

A resident of Killarney having long talked of the beautiful
vegetation he had viewed when travelling along the mountain
horse-tracks to the heads of the Condamine, Koreelah Creek,
and back by Spring Creek, inspired me with a wish to
examine the flora of the district; which, being out of the way of
most "weed collectors"—as science-despising people are apt to
dub followers of the goddess of nature, I fancied would probably
yield up something new to science. However, I am disappointed
in this respect in the phanerogamic collection I have made,
though many plants were not to be despised for they presented
greater variation than they do in the immediate Warwick district.
I may mention that through F. M. Bailey's (Colonial Botanist)
kindness I have been able to locate most or all of those collected,
though some specimens of the lower orders of cryptogamic flora
have been submitted to European specialists, the results of
whose scrutiny it will be interesting to know. A year or two
ago Mr. Bailey made a visit to the Killarney district, and,
examining the plants in the immediate vicinity, wrote two
interesting papers on the subject to the *Queenslander*. I am
not aware that he penetrated more than eight miles from the
township, so that some of the members of our Society may be
interested in the change in the larger area collected over. On
travelling up the bed of the main stream the noticeable vegetation
is almost entirely confined to timber trees, such as the scribbly,
white, or swamp gum (E. hæmastoma) a very large though
useless tree growing chiefly on its banks ; the yellow-jacket (E.
ochrophloia), whose light crown of foliage shows plainly against
the dark straight hoop-pine (A. cunninghami), seen high up on
the mountain sides ; and the swamp oak (Casuarina glauca, var.)

Few herbs or shrubs of distinction meet the eye, amongst the exceptions being Eclipta platyglossa, whose trailing stems and small yellow flowers occur in all damp gullies, and a beautiful red and purple blotched orchid (Dipodium punctatum) which grows erect in the tall blady rushes of the creek bank. Swainsona fraseri, with membraneous foliage and light bluish flowers, was also very noticeable, together with Aneilema gramineum, resembling the fringed violet minus the fringe. After a few miles rough travelling there is a change in the soil formation to such a rufous tint that one might fancy he were entering " Redmudsky" —naturally also the vegetation is slightly different. Casuarina torulosa, the forest oak, Banksia integrifolia in fruit, the Brisbane box Tristania conferta, and the black wattles—Acacia implexa and longifolia, were all also very common. As we approach the border in every gully is a trickling stream with brackens (Pteris sp.), on its banks, the most sluggish being reddened over with a small but pretty alga. On arriving at the head of Koreelah Creek and examining its various tributaries wending their way into New South Wales, I found Myriophyllum variæfolium, the large erect species, and Haloragis tetragyna ; and here upon the forest oaks grew Loranthus longiflorus, one of the mistletoes, with pinkish-white flowers. A pretty pink grass-leaved Stylidium was conspicuous, as were also the ground-ivy-leaved Goodenia (G. hederacea), the large fœtid flowered Hibbertia volubilis, only now ripening its fruit, the little shrub, Hibbertia labillardièri, with its small and pleasantly scented yellow flowers, not more than three lines in diameter ; Cassia mimosoides, with leaves almost as sensitive as those of Mimosa pudica, whose name it bears ; a species of shrubby acacia resembling in form of phyllodis that dedicated to J. H. Maiden, having at this time neither flower nor fruit ; and a dwarf Grevillea (silky oak) of gregarious habit, about 4ft. high, the leaves much broader than the common silky oak (G. robusta). Now surmounting a steep portion of the road we pass over to the Condamine drainage, and enter a dense, heavily-timbered scrub, the track barely wide enough for the horses to force their way through. We have hardly time to collect, but manage to find and secure specimens of Elæocarpus cyaneus, a shrub known in all your coast scrubs, but bearing here only small fruit ; a tree-like form of heath, Trochocarpa laurina, with beautiful small white flowers in racemes, and wheel-like fruit ; Lynoum glandulosum, with large orange-yellow bilobed fruit ; the handsome shrubby, prickly-leaved legume, Oxylobium trilobatum, with small, oblong, convex pods, bursting at the apex ; a form of Prostanthera ovalifolia ; a labiate, Bacularia monostachya (the Kentia monostachya of Bailey's Synopsis) ; and the pretty walking-stick palm which was very abundant in both flower and fruit. The trunks of the larger timber trees, such as the species of Ficus, Cedrela, and Eucalyptus, were festooned with the climbing ferns, Polypodium tenellum and P. scandens ; while acres of ground were covered with a coarse form of Blechnum cartilagineum up to the horses' girths. Here on the rocks by a clear rivulet was the pretty little filmy fern Hymenophyllum tunbridgense, in fructification; there, were met with close at hand the mosses Rhizogonium spiniforme, Leucobryum candidum, Meteorium amblyacis, Hypnodendron arcuatum, and H. curvato-comosum, Dicranum dicarpum, Porotrichum vagum, Fabronia brachydonta and the pretty hepatic, Noteroclada conflueus ; and on a tree (Eugenia smithii, which, by the way, had ripe "lily-pillies" on at the time) was the large lichen, Sticta camario and a beautiful species as yet undetermined, golden-green with black apothecia ; and at its base that large moss, Dawsonia polytrichoides, resembling when fresh a young fir-tree. Crossing the watershed to the head of Spring Creek—a Condamine feeder—the first tree-fern (Dicksonia youngiæ), comes into view, soon to be followed with as beautiful a prospect as one can imagine, thousands and thousands of these ferns lining the banks of the creek for three miles from its source downwards, and so closely packed as to impede anyone travelling through them. In front and stretching away to Killarney down the mountain slopes, are immense tracts of timber-land yielding the mahogany, black-jacket, messmate, tallow-wood, blue gum, silky oak, hoop pine, red cedar, and many other timbers supplied by the Killarney mills to the various markets. In the numerous creeks and gullies from here to Killarney were seen the elderberry-leaved Panax ; Verreaux's croton, both in flower and fruit ; the myrtle-leaved Eugenia ; and Eupomatia laurina, an anonaceous plant, the petals of which fall off by circumscissile dehiscence in the form of a

cap or calyptra. The bases of the falls were thickly carpeted
with the urticas, Elatostemma reticulatum in flower—with its
queer lop-sided leaf, and a large-leaved form of Australina
pusilla, the leaves being twice the size of those mentioned in
Gaudichaud's diagnosis. Leptospermum flavescens, a myrtaceous
plant, was here also in ripe fruit, together with Ehretia acuminata,
with its large panicles of small berries ; the twining convolvulus,
Polymeria marginata, was also in flower and fruit ; as was also
the very large trailer, Cocculus moorei, having its leaves over a foot
long and nearly as broad, while the flower sprays are barely two
inches long. The ferns, Aspidium aculeatum and Davalia dubia,
were growing with Polypodium aspidioides by the running water
together with the pretty prismatic rush, Juncus prismatocarpus,
and Chloris truncata, a star grass. It would hardly do to leave
this without mentioning the various tree, rock, and terrestrial
orchids seen on Spring Creek. Of the first were two Bul-
bophylla, namely, B. aurantiacum and B. exiguum, the latter a
minute species, with flowers scarcely visible ; and Liparis
cœlogynoides (as far as can be determined from the description
given by Baron Mueller), was noticed growing in densly-packed
rows on the tree branches, and having the pseudo bulbs angular
by mutual pressure. The dagger-leaf Dendrobium was found
on wet rocks in mid-stream, but presented neither flower nor fruit ;
while on the scrub soil occurred several plants of Calanthe
veratrifolia, in full bloom, having the summit of the scape, from
2 feet to 3 feet high, crowned with large waxy-white flowers.
It is one of our most handsome orchids.

[NOTE.—The papers referred to, as being contained in the
" Queenslander " (1891), are entitled " Botanising at Killarney,"
and are to be found in the November 14th and November 21st
issues of that journal. References should also be made to a
series of articles by C. J. Gwyther—" Botanising near Warwick,"
printed in " Queenslander," January-April, 1892.—ED.]

INJURIOUS MARINE ANIMAL.

BY

HENRY TRYON.

(Presented 2nd February, 1893).

THE *Townsville Bulletin* of the 17th January, 1885, records the death of a boy named Kiernan, who, it is stated, succumbed within five or six minutes from the time that attention was attracted by his screams, from having whilst bathing come into contact " with some marine monster." When first noticed, he was " covered with a substance somewhat resembling cobwebs," and his right side " was marked with purple weals, as if he had been beaten severely with a sharp thong." This incident was, it would appear, not a solitary one, for (to quote my authority), " the circumstances of this case show that it is a repetition of the one which occurred some short time back at Ross Island." On the 26th January, and on the 23rd February, 1885, the same journal also published further instances of the very serious consequences resulting from contact with some marine animal to bathers in the sea there, the patients being reported as having seared lines upon their skins, and exhibiting pronounced constitutional disturbances.

Being persuaded that the matter required investigation, that the medical practitioner might have something on which to base his treatment, should the urgency of the symptoms arising in future cases demand his intervention, opportunity for prosecuting the needful inquiry has been long looked for. Recently a bather at Cleveland, as we have been informed by the local press, has had still another of these painful encounters, with what in his case has been styled an " electric eel," and this circumstance, affording the occasion desired, has prompted these remarks.

Mr. H. Moar, the afflicted party in this case, informs me that, whilst resident at Cleveland, Moreton Bay, he was bathing, at about six o'clock on the morning of 15th January, in an enclosure, the walls of which—somewhat out of repair—were formed of stakes driven into the ground, and that he was standing splashing, with his arms level with the water. Suddenly he felt a shock, and experienced a sharp, burning sensation on one arm, and being thus directed to the latter noticed a long attenuated grayish-black slimy object twined in a serpentine manner nearly around it. One end of this body was free, and the other passed continuously without alteration of form into the water. With two fingers connected with the other arm he then detached it, letting it fall back into its native element. Feeling now increased pain, and sickness coming over him, Mr. Moar hastened from the water to the bathing-house close at hand. This he regained, but before he could fasten a single garment about him he found that his fingers were failing, and the sickly sensation becoming more pronounced, and being in great pain, he immediately left it to seek assistance. But he had not gone more than 30 feet from the door before he had to cling to a railing, as pain was now passing down his back, and he felt that he was "going fast." A faint cry, which was all that he could utter, brought Mr. W. Rowney and his companions, who happened to be close at hand, to his assistance. By this time the pain and loss of power had passed from his back to his legs, so that he became perfectly helpless, being unable even to prostrate himself, much less move. He was now placed on the ground, and experienced a succession of shocks (which he likened to repeated heavy discharges from an electric battery) passing from his body down his legs to his feet, and was in such agonising pain that he could not bear to be touched. Being carried to his temporary residence and placed in bed, he suffered in a similar manner till nearly noon, when he commenced to feel better. The same sensations were experienced for some days, but gradually diminished in intensity. When interviewed by me on 21st January I found the mark upon his arm as represented in the photograph exhibited (kindly furnished by Poul C. Poulsen). It measured about 18 inches in length. It even then was very conspicuous, and there was some excoriation; in fact, it presented all the appearance of a surface burn. The subject of the injury is a man of good physique, splendid health, and temperate habits, and not one likely to be influenced by a sense of fear.

The Press descriptions relating to Mr. Moar's experience and the facts which had now been elicited at once suggested the probability of the long simple tentacles of one of the Siphonophora, as for example, Physalia, the well-known Portuguese Man-of-War, being instrumental in producing the injury referred to, and this view regarding its origin, was further supported by the characters presented by the lesion produced, which was in the form of a long, narrow, gradually tapering, tortuous and obscurely transversely barred. These tentacles are essentially long, vigorous, muscular, extensile tubules, which, as Hæckel informs us, may have a length of a yard or more when contracted, but which may be extended at the will of their possessor to a length of sometimes twenty yards. They serve the purpose of capturing instruments, and offensive or defensive weapons, and may readily get detached. And the mechanism to which they owe their capabilities in these respects reside in special organs, the possession of which has led the Portuguese Man-of-War to be referred to as "dangerously poisonous." Viewing one side of this fishing tentacle we find it almost continuously occupied and embraced by reniform bodies, the outer wall of each of which contains a cushion or battery, composed largely of urticating cells of microscopic dimensions. These peculiar tissue cells (cnidoblasts) have external projections (cnidocils), and contain specially formed capsules or sacs. These capsules, which bear the name of thread-cells (nematocysts), present the following structural characters :—The cell proper consists of two membranes, and is open at one pole, where there is a relatively long hollow ingrowth in the form of a tube which has its axial portion continued in an exceedingly slender filament, which, being many times the length of the sac which includes it, is normally coiled up. The sac also contains an homogeneous fluid, which is said to be of a highly irritant nature. These nettle cells—as R. von Lendenfeld relates—are connected by a granular peduncle, which is really a nerve fibre, with a subjacent layer of nerve ganglia. And when the above projection (cnidocil) comes or is brought into contact with a foreign body, a stimulus is conveyed to the external network of muscular fibres forming the outer membrane of the urticating cell, the latter contracts, and by a sudden discharge the tube and slender filament—being first everted—is projected outwards, bathed with the fluid contents of the cell which has enclosed it, and adheres to the object that has occasioned its activity.

A professional friend, the veteran Dr. George Bennett, of Sydney, furnishes the following graphic account of the effects due to contact with Physalia, which, as it supports my contention, may now be profitably introduced. " Having captured," he writes (" Wanderings," vol. i., page 9, London, 1834), " a very fine specimen of this animal—namely, the Portuguese Man-of-War, on a former voyage, and being aware of the pungent property residing in the tentaculæ, I was desirous of trying its effects on myself, for the purpose of ascertaining from personal experience the constitutional irritative effects resulting from it. On taking hold of the animal it raised its tentaculæ, and stung me on the second and ring fingers. The sensation was similar at first to that produced by the nettle ; but before a few minutes had elapsed, a violent aching pain succeeded, affecting more severely the joints of the fingers, the stinging sensation at the same time continuing at the part first touched by the acrid fluid. On cold water being applied, with the intention of removing or lessening the pain, it was found rather to increase than diminish the effects. The irritation resulting from the poisonous fluid emitted by the animal extended upwards, increasing in extent and severity (apparently acting along the course of the nerves), and in the space of a quarter of an hour the effect in the forearm (more particularly felt at the inner part) was very violent, and at the elbow joint still more so. It may be worthy of remark that when the joints became affected the pain always increased. It became at last almost unbearable, and was much heightened on the affected arm being moved. The pulse of that arm was also much accelerated and an unnatural heat was felt over its whole surface. The pain extended to the shoulder joint, and on the pectoral muscle becoming attacked by the same painful sensation an oppression of breathing was occasioned, which we find similarly produced by rheumatism when it attacks that muscle, and it proved very distressing during the time that it remained. The continuance of the pain was very severe for nearly half-an-hour after which it gradually abated, but the after effects were felt during the remainder of the day in a slight degree of numbness and increased temperature of the arm. About two hours after I had been stung I perceived that a vesicle had arisen on the spot."

This, with the exception of some observations of Tilesius, quoted by Cuvier, is the only record of a precise observation met with by me, although the evil reputation of Physalia has reached my ears more than once in startling narrative. One of our members, however, Mr. H. G. Stokes, was once injured by a marine animal, which he is satisfied beyond the shadow of a doubt was a Portuguese Man-of-War. This event, since it relates to a Queensland experience, may be not inappropriately described. He was bathing at Pialba in 1885, and the facts he relates (he has not read any of the Press accounts of the Cleveland adventure), regarding his encounter render it again highly probable that the same kind of animal—i.e. a Physalia—that assailed him was the one concerned in Mr. Moar's case also. The parts of the body implicated were the left arm to across the chest. The mark produced was at first grayish-white, and this colour, after passing to fiery red, became blue. It was persistent for some days. The following symptoms were those experienced. Firstly, a sudden shock, then an intense burning pain—in the parts " stung "—such as is produced by contact of a hot iron with the skin, nausea with inclination to vomit, chattering of the teeth, shooting pains at the elbow, inability to use the affected arm, and a general loss of power, which for some hours rendered all work quite impracticable. A lad, the son of a Pialba hotel-keeper, was also " stung " whilst bathing from the same sea beach four or five days subsequent to the above event. Being by himself, the lad's cries attracted attention, and he was found on the shore in great agony, and unable to either walk or stand. Being carried to his home he in due course recovered, but a mark, similar to the one resulting from the accident in Mr. Stokes's case, remained on his skin for some days.

As has been already remarked in reference to Physalia, on the explosion of the urticating cells the tubes and their long attenuated filaments adhere to the body, which by contact has occasioned their discharge. It is reasonable, therefore, to expect to be able to detect vestiges of them on the injured skin whenever it is a Portu-

guese Man-of-War that has occasioned the lesion ; also to infer
contact with Physalia as accounting for an injury of doubtful
origin on detecting those microsopic objects on the skin, if other
circumstances accord with such an explanation.

Mr. Moar was therefore asked to permit the removal of
portions of the injured skin, though there was little hope of
success attending its examination since a few days had elapsed
since the accident, the injured part had been anointed with
turpentine and also with ammonia besides having been washed,
and had also been brought into contact with his shirt sleeve.
However, after careful examination with an objective of high
power ($\frac{1}{12}$ Gundlach), I was able to demonstrate the presence on
a particle of epidermis of the characteristic extremely fine thread
of the nematocyst of Physalia, and thus to add to my opinion the
weight due to an ascertained fact. Briefly, then, I may conclude
by stating that the injury from which Mr. Moar suffered was
occasioned, as have been in all probability, those from time to
time recorded of a similar nature, by a Portuguese Man-of-War,
and not by a hypothetical " electric eel," or " sea monster," and
the remedial measures for palliating or checking the symptoms
which supervene, are those appropriate to an injury of similar
origin.

[Note.—Whilst the above was passing through the press the
following incident was alluded to in the local press :—" On the
afternoon of Saturday, December 1st, two gentlemen were
bathing in front of Shorncliffe in about 5ft. of water, when one
felt a sharp pain on his ribs as if a red-hot iron had been placed
on it. He shouted out and plucked from his side a small kind
of jelly fish, blue in colour. As he seized it the animal flung a
thin tail nearly a yard long up his back and over his shoulder
down across the breast. The body broke off form the tail, and
he flung it away. Both gentlemen rushed into the bathing-box,
and here the tail was removed. It also was a kind of blue jelly ;
the place where the body had stuck was oval in shape, about
2½in. by 1½in. This came up into a large blister, and every
place touched by the tail also rose up like a stout cord of blister.
They at once hastily put on some clothing and rushed to where
they were staying, where the blue bag was applied every few
minutes for about an hour. For nearly two hours the person

stung suffered great pain, and in the early stage real agony.
Although the blue took away all the pain there is still a raised
cord at each spot the tail touched."—H.T.]

PLANT CLASSIFICATION.

BY

HENRY TRYON.

(Read on 20th April, 1893).

[THIS was an exposition of the system of classification
applied by Baron F. von Mueller to Australian phanerogamic
vegetation as the outcome of his own investigation and in accord-
ance with the views of the leading European continental
botanists, special attention being drawn to his distribution of
the orders embraced in Monochlamydeæ, amongst those to which
they were naturally allied, instead of maintaining them separately
as an artificial group of plants.—ED.] *Vide* " *Queenslander*,"
29th April, 1893.

GEOLOGY OF THE GLASSHOUSE MOUNTAINS.

BY

HENRY G. STOKES, F.G.S.

(Read on 18th May, 1893).

BRIEFLY to allude to what is already known concerning the
Glasshouse Mountains, it may be remarked that the literature
relating to the geology of this district is somewhat meagre
and conflicting. The following extract, bearing on the subject,
taken from a letter of Ludwig Leichhardt's, dated 4th
September, 1843, Archer Station, Bunya Bunya, appears in
" Cooksland "*: " Last Saturday I returned from a three days'
trip to the Glass Houses. . . . . . . The highest—
Beriwah—is about 1,000 feet high, and is composed of a rock
entirely different from the surrounding mountains. I have seen

* " Cooksland" : J. D. Lang, D.D., 1847.

similar mountain features in the neighbourhood of Clermont
Ferrand in the Auvergne, and geologists have called these
rocks domite, because of its affecting generally the form of a
dome. This domite belongs to the trachytic group. It is
rather an earthy paste with some scattered crystals of feldspar."

In August, 1854, Mr. Stutchbury† gave a somewhat detailed
account of these hills, ascribing their origin to local metamorph-
ism induced in the sandstone rocks of the district by some
deep-seated foci of heat, &c., subsequent denudation having
carried away the unaltered material while it could not affect the
indurated portions to the same extent, and which were therefore left undecomposed. They are regarded by the Hon. A. C.
Gregory‡ as "eruptive porphyries," and by the Rev. J. E.
Tenison-Woods§ as "prismatic basalt."

The ground traversed between the railway line and McGregor's
accommodation house consists of low sandy ridges, tea-tree flats,
and open forest country, rising gradually towards the Gympie
road, where several outcrops of a fragmental volcanic rock are
noticeable. Proceeding still further west, the scenery changes as
the level country is left behind; numerous steep ridges and
escarpments of sandstone, with gullies on each side and covered
by timber of large dimensions, run toward and parallel to
the range until the basalt spurs of the Taylor are met with. In
these gullies sandstones and shales outcrop, and numerous
fragments, of silicified wood lie scattered about the surface of
the ridges. The sedimentary rocks which are thus illustrated
belong to the Ipswich beds, and probably rest unconformably
on the schists which appear at the foot of the range to the
south. An extensive view of the surrounding country may be
obtained from the top of Beerwah, the highest and most
westerly of the Glasshouse Mountains. Looking south, between
the basalt range and the coast, the comparatively level country
presents an unbroken line of horizon, except where the isolated
peaks of the Glasshouses lying in that direction have broken
through the sandstone; this plain, stretching some thirty-five or

† N.S.W. Geol. Survey—Fourteenth Report—in Legislative Council
Papers, N.S.W., Sept., 1854.
‡ "Report on Geology of part of Districts of Wide Bay and Burnett,"
Brisbane: Government Printer, 1875.
§ Proc. Roy. Soc., N.S.W.—Vol. XXII., 1888, Plates 19 and 20.

forty miles southward, is seen to gradually close in towards the coast near Brisbane. The Glasshouse Mountains, nine in number, are contained within an area of about eight square miles. A line, four miles in length, drawn due west from the railway station, passes through Ngungun, Coonowrin (1,170 feet), and Beerwah (1,760 feet), and these are about equidistant from one another. Tunbubudla (1,020 feet) is situated four and a-quarter miles to the south of Coonowrin, and three and a-half miles further south from it is Miketeebumulgrai. Returning to Ngungun, two and a-half miles south of it, lies Tibrogargan and Ewan ; two miles to the south of these hills, Beerburrum.

They have an average elevation of 1,000 feet above sea level, Beerwah being 1,760 feet and Ewan 560 feet above " McGregor's." They also lie in two parallel lines to the coast, and possess many features in common. When viewed from a distance Coonowrin presents the appearance of a truncated cone resting on a dome-shaped base, the apex slightly overhanging to the west. The truncated portion rises abruptly on three sides showing columnar cliffs, the columns inclining inwards in places towards its summit. Its north-west flank is, however, not so steep, and here a succession of small ledges appear to offer a reasonable prospect of success to anyone who may be tempted to try the ascent. On the south-west flank of the mountain a recent landslip exposes a section illustrating the manner in which the igneous rock has pierced and involved the sedimentary rocks resting at its base, proving that the volcanic eruptions of this locality are more recent than the Ipswich beds.

Ewan resembles a Japanese fan sloping towards the range, the handle consisting of a long narrow ridge with precipitous sides, ending in a perpendicular escarpment in the opposite direction, some 560 feet above the plain. The others were not visited during our trip, but they appear from a distance to be of the same type as those already described. There is reason for concluding also that they are not only connected with each other but are in reality offshoots from the great eruptive trachytes of the Main Dividing Range, so prominent a feature in the southern portion of the Moreton district. In fact we may presume that this isolated group of hills represents the site of ancient volcanoes which burst through fissures in the sandstone and shales of the Jurassic period, and the solid plugs of trachyte which filled the throats of the original cones alone remain as evidences of their former greatness. The loose accumulations of ejected materials that we may assume at one time existed on their flanks have been stripped off and swept away during ages of denudation, only the more compact fragmental material being left at their base. Thus the ridges in the vicinity of Coonowrin and Tibberogargan, two of the principal elevations composing the Glasshouse Mountains, consist mainly of solid trachyte and trachyte-breccia, with fragments of coarse sandstone and grit strewn about the surface. The rock generally is a light coloured, rough and porous, but fine-grained variety of trachyte, rich in sanidin, with numerous needles and prisms of hornblende, plagioclase, some biotite and porphyritic blebs of quartz.

The sides of Beerwah and Coonowrin present very beautiful examples of columnar structure. Both vertical and inclined columns are present, and these are mostly hexagonal and do not appear to exceed 2 feet in diameter. As the rock also weathers unevenly in places, shallow cavernous hollows are thus formed in the more exposed sides of the mountains. Wherever conditions have been favourable for the accumulation of rock *débris* and soil, vegetation is abundant; but there are many quite naked rock exposures and escarpments. From these remarks it may be affirmed that this recent examination supports the conclusion respecting the nature and origin of these remarkable landmarks in southern Queensland previously arrived at by the ill-fated Ludwig Leichhardt.

ON THE OCCURRENCE OF A NEW DENDROCEROS IN QUEENSLAND.

BY

C. J. WILD, F.L.S.

(Read on 6th July, 1893).

Dendroceros is the name applied to one of the most interesting genera of Hepaticæ or Scale Mosses. The species hitherto met with have a somewhat remarkable range of occurrence, having been recorded from the great South American Cordillera, the island of St. Vincent and from Queensland; in fact, that now under consideration more nearly approaches an Andean form—D. foliatus, *Spruce*, than any other. These Scale Mosses seem only to have been found towards the summits of mountains, and unlike their allies—the different species of Anthoceros, Lunularia, Marchantia, &c., are strictly arboreal, growing upon the trunks of trees, usually towards their bases. Dendroceros muelleri and the present species are the sole Australian representatives of the genus, and the former of these has been collected only upon Mt. Bellenden-Ker where it was procured by Messrs. Froggatt and Sayer in 1886. As regards Dendroceros subtropicus, *mihi*, this has been found upon Mt. Tambourine and hitherto nowhere else. The following is a technical description of it :—

DENDROCEROS SUBTROPICUS, *sp. nov.*, Fronds deep green, cæspitose-procumbent, 15 lines, ascending, pinnately ramose. Costa well-defined, narrow, of several layers of cells, pagina broad, deeply cleft into broadly linear lobes, imbricate and sinuate-crispate. Cells roundish hexagonal chlorophyllose, walls thick. Monœcious; female flower situate at the base of the furcations surrounded by large crispate lobes. Capsule bivalved rufous, 7 lines long; involucre about half the length, linear, cylindrical, green, columella filiform persistent. Spores small, round, green, granulate ·05mm. Elaters smooth flat and twisted in a loose spiral ·5 x 007mm.

E

This species differs from D. crispatus in having a more exserted capsule, and the frond broader and more deeply lobed, and from D. Muelleri by the slender columella by the roundish quadrate cells of the capsule and the smooth exterior of the latter—the cells in D. Muelleri being linear oblong and those situated on the exterior of the apex swollen and bulged out. On the other hand it more nearly approaches D. foliatus, from which species it differs in wanting the broad pale costa and having a more abbreviated capsule.

SOME GLADFIELD FUNGI.

BY

C. JULIAN GWYTHER.

(Read on 6th July, 1893).

[This, which was accompanied by pencil sketches, was an account of the fungi which had been found by the author at Gladfield, in the vicinity of Warwick, during the preceding few weeks. It comprised a reference to no less than 148 species— the majority of which were briefly described. As at present it is found impracticable to reproduce the illustrations referred to, the publication of the paper, which in their absence would lose very much of its interest, is postponed.—ED.]

INSECTS AS FUNGUS HOSTS.

BY

HENRY TRYON.

(Read on 20th July, 1893).

DURING the last three months there has been more than one instance reported of caterpillars occurring in formidable numbers and doing extensive damage to growing crops, and it must have been thought by many that if even a small proportion of these arrived at the imago or perfect condition, and eggs were in turn produced, and so eventually a greatly augmented host of larvæ, the prospects of those who were dependent on the products of the soil for their livelihood would be gloomy indeed. It happens, however, that these caterpillars have terrible enemies to contend with, before whose onslaught they at times almost wholly succumb.

As a case in point it may be mentioned that quite recently numerous large ichneumon flies with red bodies and steel-blue wings, belonging to the genus Pimpla, might have been seen throughout the day in Musgrave Park, South Brisbane, passing rapidly to and fro just above the surface of the grass growing in the low-lying situations there, and ever and anon suddenly alighting and creeping amongst the herbage. Even at nightfall they were still at their posts, remaining—three or four together—stationary on the grass stems. The curious observer might further have noticed that they were in quest of fat, naked, striped grubs—the caterpillars of a noctuid moth—which in turn were present in such numbers as completely to keep the growth of the herbage in check, and that whenever one of these was discovered by the ichneumon, the latter pierced it with a formidable ovipositor, that it might yield food for a future progeny. So numerous indeed were these ichneumons that it seemed unlikely that any caterpillars would escape their attacks, notwithstanding the latter lay quiet and concealed till darkness supervened, when their depredations would commence.

In addition to such enemies as that mentioned, caterpillars and indeed other insects as well—have to contend with a much more potent agent in accomplishing their destruction.   You will remember that one of the finest rural industries of France was ruined for some years by reason of a malady that decimated the caterpillars yielding the silk of commerce, and how, after five consecutive years of laborious investigation, the renowned Pasteur arrived at the knowledge of a practical means for check-ing the evil and preventing its occurrence in the future.   On reference to his " Etudes sur la Maladie des Vers à Soie," you will find that this destruction of the silkworms of the south of France was occasioned especially by two diseases, " la pebrine " and " la flacherie," the one determined by the presence of a psorosperm and the other by that of a schizomycete or bacterium —both low forms of fungi, and giving rise to these two special diseases, which are hereditary as well as communicable. Similarly at an earlier date another silkworm disease, " l'efflores-cence," had been shown by Davaine and Robin to be due to an entomogenous fungus named then—by Balsam — Botrytis Bassiana, and afterwards Isaria destructor.

Silkworms are not the only caterpillars thus affected; nor are the latter and insects generally subject to fungus diseases only, when reared under artificial conditions. This last mentioned fungus, Isaria destructor, was early found to be communicable and to occasion disease in insects belonging to quite different genera, and even orders, than does the silkworm, and afterwards to occur in them whilst living in the open even under natural conditions. In fact, caterpillars and almost all other insects are now known to be liable to disease due to the growth of parastic fungi in or upon them.   To such an extent is this so, too, that special memoirs have been written dealing with fungi and their insect hosts, such, for example, as N. Gray's " Notices of Insects that are known to form the bases of Fungoid Parasites," Thaxter's " En-tomopthoreæ of the United States," and Krassilstschik's " De Insectorum Morbis qui fungis parasitis efficiuntur "—the last work published at Odessa in the *Zapiski* of the Naturalists' Society of New Russia.

In Australia the subject seems to have been almost wholly neglected, though a few fungi, subsisting upon living insects, have certainly been systematically determined and described. There are three species of Cordyceps—C. Gunnii, C. Hawkesii, and C. entomorrhiza—giving rise to what are known as "vegetable caterpillars." Two species of Isaria—I. cicadæ and I. suffructicosa—the former, as its name implies, from the cicada, and the latter parasitic on a living hairy caterpillar; two species of Microcera, which live on Scale Insects—one of which it was my privilege to introduce to science; an undescribed fungus already noticed by myself as having the Black Scale for its host; and, finally, the well-known parasite of the house-fly, formerly known as Sporendonema musci or Empusa musci, but now regarded as the terrestrial form of Saprolegnia ferox. None of these, however, except the last mentioned, may be regarded as virulent enemies of the species of the insects which they affect, although the species of Microcera are highly prejudicial to those particular kinds of insects which they affect.

The well-known vegetable caterpillars before you (two from New Zealand and two—involving, vine-feeding hawk-moth caterpillars—from New South Wales) illustrate what is implied by parasitism by Cordyceps. Here a larva of ordinary soft consistence has been brought into contact with or become infected by a special fungus-spore which has germinated within it, and in the course of continuous vegetative growth has completely replaced the original animal tissue by a tough white compact substance, which when examined by aid of the microscope will be found to be composed of intricately interlacing tubular bodies or hyphæ—the elementary tissue of the fungus. The caterpillar when in this condition, is hard, but quite fragile, being then easily broken across. Frequently growth does not proceed beyond this stage, but under favourable conditions reproductive organs are formed, a stout stalk-like body several inches in height arising just behind the head. This body may be simple or bifurcate, and terminate in a cylindrical or subclavate head, which will be found to be minutely dotted and rough at the sites of little pores, which mark the position of the perithecia, which contain elongated vesicles—the asci, in each of which are eight jointed filiform bodies, the spores.

As an example of a beetle-larva affected by a related fungus, there is the accompanying specimen for which I am indebted to Mr. F. Gore, of Yandilla. Here we have one of the redoubtable " white grubs," which sugar-planters know so well—the early condition of some scarabæid beetle, in a mummified condition with two contorted bodies, one simple and the other branched, springing like large horns one on either side from just behind the head.

As for the house-fly and its disease. You may almost at any time notice an example of this familiar insect adherent to the window-pane, surrounded by a pale gray cloud made up of minute particles. Whilst at a slightly anterior date the fly itself will exhibit little pale-coloured tufts which have oozed out from between the rings of the abdomen. These tufts on microscopic examination will be found to be composed of slender tubular vesicles, or " flocci," which adhere to one another, each floccus containing numerous spore-like bodies, which are in fact zoospores, being—when liberated in a suitable medium— endowed with characteristic motility. It is this fungus which checks the increase of house-flies to an extent little suspected; and which might become available when artificially cultivated not only for contending with these domestic pests, but also for checking the maggot which may be credited with the destruction of about 50 per cent. of our soft fruits.

Still another instance of fungus-parasitism may be profitably considered. A few days since some caterpillars belonging to a noctuid moth—a species of Agrotis—still attached to a lettuce leaf were officially brought under my notice, it being suggested that the lettuce had proved poisonous to them, as every caterpillar which had been found upon this plant was either already dead or in a moribund condition. Unfortunately these caterpillars when examined were, with one exception, in an advanced stage of decay, and had their bodies filled with liquid contents; but the one affording the exception was completely covered by irregular grayish tufts which produced an appearance suggestive of brain convolutions. These tufts were found to be composed of hyphæ—in some instances branched —which supported irregularly ovoid bodies, or conidia.

This fungus, found under the conditions mentioned, was with little doubt a species of Entomopthora, closely related to E. plusiæ, a fungus which Professor Giard detected in 1888 destroying the caterpillar of the silver Y moth, which in turn had been found devastating fields of lucerne and trefoil. In fact there can be little doubt but that all the caterpillars noticed upon the lettuce, as well as many others unobserved, had succumbed to the same virulent fungus disease. The green caterpillar of Plusia verticillata, one of the greatest pests of the florist, has been met with by me on more than one occasion here, hanging by its abdominal prolegs dead, discoloured, and full of fluid material, having perished from a similar cause.

These instances mentioned may be regarded as illustrations of fungus insect-parasites belonging to four different classes : the Cordyceps of the "vegetable caterpillar," representing one of the Spheriaceæ ; the fungus of the beetle-larva, the Hyphomycetæe ; that of the house-fly, the Saprolegniæ; and that of the caterpillar from the lettuce, the Entomopthoreæ or Empuseæ. They agree—as do perhaps all the disease-producing fungi— with the exception of bacteria—in the fact that each occurs in two or more different forms, though in the case of most of these referred to, the different phases have not separately been made known. These are distinguished essentially by the condition of their reproductive organs and the character of their spores. The Cordyceps of the "vegetable caterpillar" may be regarded as the ascigerous condition of an Isaria, the latter a fungus in which the spores consist not of jointed thread-like bodies, but of more or less globose ones—i.e., conidia-terminating clubs, or flocci. In the case of the muscardine of the silkworm, as we have seen, it is, on the other hand, the Isaria or conidiferous form, and not the cordyceps one, which is so destructive. The fungus of the house-fly is the imperfect terrestrial condition of Saprolegnia ferox (Kutz), a plant organism which occurs saprophytically upon dead insects in water. That of the noctuid caterpillar—Agrotis—from the lettuce, is the empusa form of a fungus, which, bearing other characters, is known as a Tarichium.

This assumption by the same plant of different forms is, in the case of these insect-infesting fungi, influenced by conditions

of environment, the nature of which has in many cases yet to
be investigated or even discovered, but that these conditions are
not exclusively climatic in their nature has been definitely
ascertained. Taking the case of these fungi, which may be considered as species of Entomopthora, or close allies, it has been
ascertained that the two forms may occur on the same insect
simultaneously, and this is true of fungi of this genus occurring
in insect hosts belonging to such distinct categories as do caterpillars and grasshoppers. Again, in the case of others the
different phases make their appearance at different times of the
year. Further, what is still more remarkable, one form seems
occasionally to be restricted to a particular geographical zone.
As an instance of this, it may be mentioned that Krassilstschik
reports that whereas the Entomopthora which destroys the " cut-
worms " of the wheat—Agrotis segetum — at Odessa always
occurs in the conidial form, according to Cohn it is met with
exclusively in the Tarichium condition in the widely separated
region to which his investigations relate. Though again the two
forms may be confined to the same kind of insect it happens not
rarely that quite different insects may serve as the respective hosts.
And what is more remarkable still, there is an Entomopthora
(E. calliphoræ), as Professor Giard has informed me, occurring
in a fly, which has only been met with as a parasitic fungus in
the phase in which resting-spores occur, and these spores present special peculiarities which are exactly repeated in a fungus,
which hitherto has been found exclusively on the fæcal matter
of frogs and lizards, which are known to be very partial to the
flies of the same genus Calliphora—these reptiles often containing the resting-spores of the fly parasite in their digestive organs
in an incipient stage of growth. As it might have been inferred
these conidia and resting-spores, separately characteristic of the
two phases in the fungus growth, in addition to their distinct
morphological characters are widely different in their behaviour
as living objects. The former germinate readily; the patho-
logical conditions which they give rise to are communicated with
facility through their agency to other insects, but they themselves quickly perish. On the other hand, the resting-spores
have their vitality persistent, but cannot be made to germinate
artificially even when kept under apparently suitable conditions

as regards warmth and moisture for a lengthened period, and from the foregoing observation relating to the Entomopthora of the fly—it has been suggested that the intervention of quite another substance—serving as host—is needed for continuous development, and that many of these insect parasites have phases of existence, one as saprophytes and the other as insect-haunting plants: or, in other words, that their parasitism is merely facultative.

The communicability of a fungus disease, due to the presence of an Entomopthora in its conidia-bearing condition, from insect to insect, has been mentioned, and it remains to state that, in the light of recorded observation, the same is possible in the case of those dependent on the presence of other entomogenous fungi, especially such as belong to the group Isariæ, which, as has been remarked, represents the conidial condition of the ascigerous Cordyceps or Torrubium—illustrated by the vegetable caterpillars on exhibition. And it is interesting to recall the fact that the experiments which demonstrated this communicability were undertaken with a view to the discovery whether or not these fungus enemies of insects might be used as remedial agents in contending with some of the more intractable pests with which the agriculturist has to contend ; savants reflecting that, whereas such fungi were certainly inimical to the growth or even continued existence of certain industries, and especially to that of silk culture, and so should be held in check ; there were, on the other hand, a host of insects which, by their depredations, largely militated against the success of other enterprises, especially the ones connected with agriculture, and that it would be largely to the interest of those concerned with such pursuits if these fungi might be made available in fighting them. Thus the celebrated Russian scientist, Metschnikoff, having become aware that the fungus Isaria destructor preyed upon the " white grub " of the scarabæid beetle, Anisophia austriaca, which in the south of Russia ravaged the wheatfields, and knowing that it could be transferred from grub to grub, conceived the idea of cultivating this fungus apart from its host in some artificial medium, and so arming himself with a powerful instrument for contending with this destructive beetle in the many regions where the Isaria

fungus did not already occur. This savant then, aided by
Cienkowsky, as early as 1879, accomplished the result at which
he had aimed, employing as a nutrient medium a fluid composed
of the fermented juice of the maize. A correspondent, Professor
Alfred Giard, Chargé d'Cours in connection with the Faculty of
Science at the Sorbonne, to whom I am indebted for much of
the information contained in this paper, about the same time
experimented with entomogenous fungi, belonging to the class
Entomopthora, but was not, however, able to cultivate them
artificially apart from the insects on which they were naturally
met with, or to which they had been communicated. He was,
however, subsequently successful with Isaria densa, which lives
on the *ver blanc*, another destructive scarabæid larva ; and this
fungus, which was thus found to be capable of being artificially
cultivated, was also discovered to be available for the direct
infestation of no less than twenty-four different kinds of other
insects.

Again, a most encouraging instance of the utilisation of
these fungus diseases in fighting insect pests is that afforded by
the experiments of F. H. Snow, entomologist to the Kansas
State Board of Agriculture, with the fungi found infesting the
well-known Chinch Bug (Blissus leucopterus) of the United
States. This insect harbours three plant parasites—a white
fungus (Entomopthora or Empusa), a bacterial disease (Micrococcus), and a fungus regarded as an Isaria or Trichoderma—all
of which may be found co-existing on the same individual. In
Mr. Snow's experiments, specimens of the Chinch bug, dead from
fungus disease, were confined with about twenty times their
number of healthy ones from the field, for forty-eight hours, and
the resulting sick insects, which by this time had become
infested, were liberated in fields wherein the pest was prevalent,
and by this means the latter was kept in subjection, if not
almost stamped out. And so generally recognised were the good
results accruing that Mr. Forbes, at the time of writing,
intimated that no less than seventeen hundred applications for
diseased Chinch bugs had been received at his laboratory, and
that the malady had been introduced from it into Missouri,
Nebraska, Indiana, Ohio, and Minnesota.

In introducing the subject of fungus parasites, mention was made of the diseases in silkworms due to bacteria, or the lowest class of these organisms, and it may be remarked in conclusion that bacteria seem equally available with, if not more so than, these higher forms as aids in contending with insect pests of vegetation. Micrococcus occasioning a virulent affection in the cabbage white butterfly of Europe and America has been long since isolated, but investigations with a view to determine its efficacy for the purpose mentioned have scarcely proceeded as yet beyond the experimental stage, and at the hands of Brefeld better results have attended the employment of the conidial form of the Empusa peculiar to the caterpillar of that insect. Perhaps, however, the most recent inquiry in this direction is that conducted by Mr. F. W. Malley, Assistant Entomologist to the United States Department of Agriculture, with a view to discover whether the germs often pathogenic in the notorious " Boll Worm "—Heliothris armiger—a Queensland insect, might not be utilised as a so-called remedial agent. As yet his investigations have not led to any very practical results ; but amongst other conclusions at which he arrived, he ascertained that from production by artificial means of disease by a fungus germ in one species of insect, it did not necessarily follow that in all cases the same germ could in like manner be employed to originate a disease in a closely related species, much less in one more distantly related. In the case of the bacteria of this Boll Worm, to which his attention was especially directed, he found that their parasitism in relation to it was only facultative, and that they were otherwise saprophytic, or lived on dead substances of animal origin, and that as a primary condition for arriving at a successful issue, it was necessary in the case of experiments with a living germ—whether actually parasitic or only faculta- tively parasitic—to discover all its relations to environment which allowed of its producing disease. The subject has, however, perhaps been pursued far enough this evening. It is hoped that sufficient has been stated to show that the study of the disease of insects is a matter not altogether devoid of interest.

THE STRAWBERRY DISEASE.

HENRY TRYON.

(Read on 5th October, 1893).

THIS paper related to the features presented by a special strawberry disease of not infrequent occurrence in Southern Queensland, occasioned by the attacks of a fungus parasite, Sphærella fragariæ, the morphological characters of which were also dilated upon.—(*Abstract*). *Vide* " *Queenslander*," 21st October, 1893.

THREE UNDESCRIBED INSECTS WHOSE FOOD-PLANT IS THE MORETON BAY FIG AND THE INJURIES WHICH THEY OCCASION.

BY

HENRY TRYON.

(Read on 19th October, 1893).

SOME three month since our hon. secretary, Mr. R. Illidge, drew attention to certain lepidopterous insects which, in their caterpillar phase, fed upon the foliage of the Moreton Bay fig, and I will now introduce to the notice of those present several insects belonging to other orders which are very harmful to the same plant.

The first to mention is the homopterous insect, Psylla fici (H.T.). A curious appearance has of late years characterised some examples of the species of native fig grown for ornamental or shade purposes in different parts of our metropolis, and especially so the Moreton Bay fig—Ficus macrophylla. Large dark-brown opaque more or less glossy scab-like bodies, composed of a viscid glutinous substance, have appeared on the under surfaces of the leaves, the leaf-tissue at and around these spots has become brown and dead, and the leaves themselves have eventually dropped off whilst still green. Sometimes but one of these bodies is present on a leaf; oftentimes, however, five or six; and as for size they vary from ¼in. to 2in. across. So prevalent is the affection that in many cases trees have been completely denuded of their foliage. Some of them have, however, been fortunately able to develop terminal shoots and so commence afresh their vegetative growth; others, too debilitated through loss of their assimilative organs to do so, have emitted frail lateral offsets, which in turn have either become covered with a curious dwarfed foliage or have even also perished. In many trees, as a consequence, the symmetry of form has been permanently affected; in all, the growth has been seriously retarded.

This injury is due to the attacks of a small transparent four-winged snout-bearing jumping insect referable to the order Homoptera and the genus Psylla, measuring obout two lines in length. Its inimical relation to the fig tree, on which it subsists, will be seen from the following particulars concerning its life history.

The eggs are laid side by side, in groups of from five to a hundred—or even more, on the under surface of the leaf. They are small oval dull-brown objects, having each a central ridge and a beak-like downwardly-directed process—the extremity of which is the point of attachment. Owing to their colour and the number which each group comprises, the latter are conspicuous objects. Several groups generally occur on each leaf or the entire margin may be bounded by them, and thus the eggs present on a single leaf may amount to some thousands.

In hatching the egg splits open along the dorsal keel, and the young one to which it gives birth is wingless and active. This is a parallel-sided six-legged reddish-yellow insect, rounded in front and behind. A curved line separates an anterior smooth from a posterior segmented portion. The former, in addition to the six legs, bears two bright red lateral eye-spots. The most conspicuous feature in the ringed portion is afforded by two orifices—the dorsal spinnerets, one on each side near the hinder border, and from each of these the insect emits con-

tinuously a relatively thick ultimately opaque and white thread.
As, too, the insects when in this larval state, though active, do
not move far from one another, these threads soon interlace, and
thus the leaf appears to have white glistening objects scattered
over its green surface. The insects now soon insert their
probosces into the leaf-tissue, after which event they probably
move but little. They now, too, elaborate from the milky plant-
juice and excrete an extremely viscid and tenacious substance
which, however, does not adhere to their own bodies since these
are covered by this time with a mealy secretion. This glutinous
substance becomes blended with the foregoing threads and forms
a compact low canopy beneath which the insects, arising from
each group—or conjoined groups—of eggs feed. It, moreover,
day-by-day, becomes more extensive, elevated, and darker. The
insects after several ecdeses, or changes of the skin, eventually
cease feeding and become active pupæ. In this pupal condition
they resemble the larvæ, but possess conspicuous wing-cases as
an additional feature. The pupæ after a while crawl out from
beneath their covering and may be found scattered all around it,
usually within a distance of half-an-inch. And from them the
perfect or winged insects emerge through a longitudinal opening
behind the head. It now resembles a miniature cicada, and has
its wings placed perpendicularly along the sides of the body, and
extending some distance beyond its hindmost extremity. The
head is very broad and bent downwards beyond the large
protuberant lateral eyes. It has a stout jointed proboscis and
ten-jointed antennæ. These have their two short basal joints
yellow, but are in other respects black. The hind part of the
thorax supports two blunt tubercles. The hind body is six-
jointed. The legs are yellow, and the leg-joints of the hindmost
pair have at their extremity six little spines which assist the
insect in leaping. On the least disturbance the adult Psylla
springs from its support, takes wing, but quickly alights again.

It would seem that as the eggs are freely exposed they
might readily be destroyed by the application of insecticides.
It happens, however, that their shells are very thick and
impervious, so that kerosene emulsion may be sprayed upon
them with little or no appreciable effect. The adult insects are,

however, readily destroyed, but owing to their restless disposition can with difficulty be reached. Fortunately, however, the larva is pursued by a small bright metallic hymenopterous insect with lance-shaped hind body and short ovispositor. This parasite lays its egg within or upon the young Psylla. At the present time the eggs of the Psylla upon the leaves of our Moreton Bay figs are in process of hatching, and it is an interesting sight to notice these little friendly insects moving stealthily amongst the destructive larvæ with wings folded back depositing their eggs one by one in them, the latter as yet for a short time unprotected by their glutinous secretions.

2. The second injurious insect is a beetle which when adult drills a round hole in the young shoot just below the terminal bud and feeds its way upwards through the centre of the wood. Growth is consequently retarded, and the shoot breaks off. Neither this injury nor the insect which occasions it seems ever to have been remarked. The latter belongs to a family of very notorious timber-destroying insects—namely, the Scolytidæ; and may probably prove to belong to an undescribed genus allied to Phlœtribus. It is a very stout, short, parallel-sided, dark purplish-brown beetle, having an obscure light-coloured band widely bounding the thorax behind. It measures about ⅙in. in length. It is probably equally destructive in its larval condition, but its early stages have not as yet been observed.

3. A third destructive insect from the Moreton Bay fig also belongs to the order of beetles. It is a remarkable member of the Anthribidæ related to Montrouzier's genus Proscoporhinus, hitherto found only in New Caledonia. A curious feature in it is the excessive length of the antennæ in the male sex, these organs measuring five times the length of the body. It has also the strange habit of leaping considerable distances. Unlike the last-mentioned insect, it is during its larval condition that it carries on its depredations. The specimens shown were bred from pieces of recently dead wood; but as these were derived from trees which were previously injured by the Psylla, it is believed that the beetles are not the primary cause of the destruction of the branches in which they occurred. No doubt, however, they determine the death of many parts of the tree which but for their attacks would recover.

THE OCCURRENCE OF THE GENUS APUS IN AUSTRALIA.

BY

HENRY TRYON.

(Read on 19th October, 1893).

ALTHOUGH three species of an allied genus of entomostracon (Lepidurus) were known as existing in Australia, the genus, represented by the specimens exhibited, was an addition to its recorded fauna. Apus was in appearance a minia-ture king crab (Limulus). The Australian species measured 2in. in length ; and, when viewed from above, presented the following features :—First, there was a large oval convex shield or buckler, which sloped away on each side from a median ridge. This had the fore border rounded and bent under, whilst the hind one presented a broad and deep excavation, the sides of which were finely serrate. Beyond this shield the gradually tapering segmented hindbody extended some distance, terminat-ing in two long jointed stiff filaments or styles. At about a fourth of the length behind the fore border was a transverse groove, in front of which were two compound eyes. This con-spicuous shield was only attached to the body, which it covered, from the transverse groove forwards. On the under surface of the crustacean the antennæ, or feelers, and mouth organs were observable, and behind these no less than sixty pairs of foliaceous, or leaf-like, appendages, packed side by side, of each of which a glandular body or branchia, denotive of the respiratory function which it subserved, formed a portion. These appendages towards the forepart of the body were somewhat leg-like in appearance, but there were no true legs present. It had been computed that the segments constituting the head and body numbered twenty-six. Apus progagated commonly without the intervention of the male, this sex being very rarely met even in spots where the animal was exceedingly abundant. It was also regarded as illustrating a very old type of crustacean and on referring to the fossil Phyllopoda of the palæozoic formations of

Great Britain, figured in the Transactions of the Palæonto-graphical Society, one was at once struck with the general conformity between the figures representing the different species of Ceratiocaris and the specimens exhibited. But they were giants in those days. The number, twenty-six, given as that of the segments comprising the head and body, was two in excess of the number for the corresponding parts in the generality of living crustaceans, yet many Crustacea of the cretaceous and earlier geological formations exhibited this greater numerical development of their segments. Again, though Apus, and its ally Lepidurus, greatly differed in appearance from the other members of their class, yet they strangely recalled the Zoea condition of the common crab, or that phase exhibited immediately on hatching from the egg, which according to the principles of evolution represented an ancestral form of that familar crustacean. The very general distribution of the species of Apus over the earth's surface was, too, what might have been expected of an animal which had come into existence when time was young. The Society was indebted to Dr. T. L. Bancroft for an opportunity of exhibiting the specimens. These had been procured by Mr. G. Drew, at Wompah, in the south-western corner of the colony, where this crustacean was found plentifully frequenting the clay pans. *Abstract.*—H.T.

Note.—Mr. Lower, in commenting upon the subject, referred to an allied form found not uncommonly in the neighbourhood of Adelaide, and which was named Lepidurus angasi, a figure representing which had been exhibited by Mr. Tryon. Dr. T. P. Lucas also described a similar crustacean from the Murray district, and sought an explanation of the fact that these forms of life appeared suddenly after rain in spots which had been previously baked hard by the sun.—ED.

F

PARTIAL DECADE OF THE WARWICK ACACIAS.

BY

C. JULIAN GWYTHER.

(Read on December 7th, 1893).

In dealing with the " Wattles " of the Warwick district one
finds few that could be worked commercially as a profitable
venture, only one out of J. H. Maiden's seven valuable tan-bark
producers, namely, Acacia decurrens var. mollis, Wild., growing
naturally in the locality, and though this occurs in very fair
quantities in some portions within easy reach of a market, the
available supply is gradually being diminished, and in lieu of further
plantations, which as yet there are no signs of, must very soon
disappear altogether, especially when we remember that acres
are felled and burnt off the land, as an encumbering valueless
quantity in the eyes of selectors.   Large natural plantations of
this valuable tree are now standing bare and leafless on the
Main Range slopes, only 20 or 25 miles from Warwick, stripped
of their bark, and there is no likelihood of these waste lands being
replanted for many years to come.   There are hundreds of acres
of stony and hilly country close to Warwick of no possible use
as arable or pasture land, which might be   seeded   down
with   this   tree,   to   bring·   in   an   easily   acquired   revenue
in   half   a   dozen   years'   time.   All   the   remaining   varieties
found in the district may be classed as secondary or useless
from a commercial point of view.   The number of species known
to me is nine, which will be given in the order observed in
Bailey's " Synopsis " and Maiden's pamphlet on " Wattles and
Wattle Barks," from which latter I shall draw certain information regarding statistics and other facts.

" Acacia " of Willdenow belongs to the Sub-order Mimoseæ,
of the leguminous or bean-bearing family of the botanical world,
and in it the flower heads are grouped in—1. globular heads or
clusters ; or 2, in a cylindrical catkin-like inflorescence.   All the
Warwick varieties, with the exception of No. 9, are supplied with

rudimentary leaves, in reality merely laterally flattened leaf-stalks, termed phyllodes. A. pycnantha, Benth, a South Australian species, is *the* Acacia par excellence, as a tannic acid producer, but it is not indigenous to Queensland. Next in the scale is A. decurrens, Willd—No. 9 in the following list :—

LIST OF SPECIES REVIEWED IN THE FOLLOWING PAPER.

1. Acacia armata. R. Br.	of Secondary Quality.
2. A. salicina (var varians). Lindl.	,, ,,
3. A. linifolia. Willd.	,, ,,
4. A. decora. Reichb.	Useless
5. A. implexa. Benth.	of Secondary Quality.
6. A. melanoxylon. R. Br.	,, ,,
7. A. longifolia (var. floribunda). Willd.	,, ,,
8. A. Cunninghamii. Hook.	,, ,,
9. A. decurrens (var. mollis). Willd.	of First Quality.

A. armata, R. Br., belongs to the section " Uninerves," or acacias with single-veined phyllodia, and is a small shrub, known to most as the " Kangaroo Thorn." It is found almost everywhere in Australia on stony forest ridges such as occur at Maryvale and Rosenthal. It attains more than 12ft. here, and owing to its weakly habit of growth, about 2in. or less in diameter and is rarely found in an erect condition. The bark is smooth, very thin, easily stripped, and grey, usually marked with lighter bands, and has yielded about 3 per cent. of acid and 18 per cent. of extract, readily convincing one of its uselessness. It is also armed with stout spines ½in. long or thereabouts, which have brought it into use as a hedge plant. In November this shrub is in full fruit. The legume about 2in. long by two or three lines broad, hangs in traces along the stems from between the closely appressed semi-ovate phyllodia. The flower buds are globular on peduncles of ½in. or so, and are in bloom in August and September. As this form grows in such out of the way places and is perfectly useless commercially, little or no notice is attached to it in this district ; the only time one is apt to ascribe to it more than its share of attention is when forcing one's way through its prickly masses. This is the only spinescent form known here nearer than Stanthorpe.

2. *A.   salicina*, Lindl., or the Willow-like Acacia.
The variety represented, only one tree of which I have
observed round here, is "*varians*." This was about
15ft. high, pendulous in its manner of growth and 3in.
through the butt. The bark, which is green and smooth
on the young stems, is, when old, dark brown, brittle, rough
with longitudinal striations and is transversely furrowed as to
appear tessellated ; the wood when young is white and brittle in
the heart, but tougher just beneath the bark, showing fibrous
structure. The young stems are angular, somewhat helicoid, the
young shoots light green ; phyllodia alternate, from 5 to 8 or 9
inches long ¼ to ½in. wide, linear, lanceolate, tapering at both
ends ; the petiole short, thickened and twisted so as to bring the
upper leaf margin against the stem, one central nerve rather
prominent with hidden oblique secondary ones towards the nerved
margins, bearing from two to as many as five glands on the upper
one ; glands sometimes circular, sometimes horse-shoe shaped
and sessile ; the margin raised somewhat and almost toothed to
support the gland.

In consistency the phyllode is thick, green, fleshy, brittle,
and glandularly dotted. Panicles from 2in. to a foot in length.
Flower heads large ½ to ¾in. across, light yellow, solitary, lateral
and axillary in terminal, somewhat pendulous, leafy panicles.
Flowers usually about 20-merous ; sessile, a minute membranous
bract between each ; calyx, enclosing the base of the corolla, of
about 5 minute, almost invisible, green teeth at summit, the
whole one line in length ; corolla tube of 5 minute green teeth,
of half a line each, connected at the base into a tube two lines
long : receptacle ovate, pitted and marked with black,
stamens connected in a bundle round the ovary, composed of
whitish capillary filaments 4 to 6 lines long and often
flexuose; cellular, wrinkled near the summit and much contracted
directly below the anthers, which are small, yellow, two-celled,
peltate, two-lobed, and squarish. Style four lines, white, fila-
mentous, flexuose or straight, not exserted beyond the staminal
filaments, composed of cylindrical cells, placed rather laterally
at the summit of the ovary which in its turn is one line long,
glabrous, greenish, obovate, and is under the lens minutely

pitted. Legume singiy, or in twos or threes, 4in long by five or six lines broad and as much as three thick, sometimes constricted between the seeds and usually inflated or thickened over them, there being five or six or more to each pod, which, when green, is brittle, very thick and fleshy, and well supplied with a sticky extremely bitter juice, probably containing saponin. The dry pods are brown and woody, with a rough outer membrane; the bean, when full grown, but still unripe, is a glossy white, ovate, placed longitudinally in the pod, and is attached to, at first, a filiform colourless funicle, somewhat flexuose, but becoming finally a dark orange-red folded two or three times and clasping the entire base of the seed.

In length it is four or five lines long by three wide and thick. This species is known under the various local names of "Native Willow," "Cooba" or "Koubah" of N.S.W., Baku of Rockhampton; and Motherumba. Its full dimensions in N.S.W. are from 20 to 40 feet high and 18in. diameter; in a mature tree the bark is usually flaky, hard, and very rugged but not fibrous; from ¾ to 1in. thick and compact, it is altogether a very promising dry country bark with an acid percentage of 13 to 15 and 33 of extract, and as a secondary bark would be well worth conserving. The blacks understand the value of its bark as they preserve wallaby and other skins by its agency. The only specimen seen in the district grew in loose, loamy scrub soil; flowering in March, with full grown green legumes in October. Bailey says of the seeds that they are oblique the funicle extending up one side.

3. *A. linifolia*, Willd., or the Flax-leaved Acacia, is one of the commonest species of the Downs, though more specially observable on the hilly and scrubby country. It grows to a beautifully shrubby tree 25 feet high and 8 or 10 inches through, attaining this dimension in rich scrub soil in about five years. The immense quantity of foilage and bloom at certain seasons, when weighted down by a shower of rain, is often detrimental to the tree, causing it to split apart. It is very rare that a full-sized tree has not been damaged in this way. When in full bloom in July or January (it always flowers twice a year, though the midwinter crop does not mature seed in any

quantity, and what does mature is apt to be worked upon by an insect and galled), the tree is an object of indescribable beauty, being one graceful feathery golden mass, the bloom so closely covering the entire branches as to preclude all signs of leaf foliage. The bark, as noticed on our trees, has a reddish-grey tinge, is thin and fibrous, and externally is generally smooth, not flaky. An Enoggera sample analysed in 1891 yielded only 11 per cent. of tannic acid, with 28 per cent. of extract. In scrubby land the plant only attains to a few feet and of such dimensions as be of no use unless for extract, should it pay to send to market. The phyllodia of the plant are barely two inches long, tapering much at the base, the tips also are very pointed, one nerved, about three lines wide, margins sometimes ciliate, with a gland above the base. The whole inflorescence forms large leafy panicles covering the entire ends of the branches for two or three feet, and is formed of short racemes (two or three inches) with numerous alternate flower-heads, each containing fifteen or twenty buds though sometimes much less; at the base of each flower-head is a minute triangular bract, the back and summit of which contain a tuft of 3 or 4-celled hairs. The staminal filaments are very flexuose, each bearing rather large, two-celled anthers, the lobes of which are slightly hollowed in the front, and burst in vertical slits. The golden pollen grains present truly lovely forms and would make attractive slides if mounted; they are flattened and circular with about sixteen parallelogrammic geometric markings. clearly visible under a low power, but with a 1¼in. objective the excessive regularity of the " squares " is marvellous. Examine a hundred or so on the slide and all are marked precisely the same. The flower heads are about three or four lines across when in full bloom. The pod is 2 to 2½ins. long by four lines broad, having a bluish tinge and is very flat, often twisting spirally before ripening and turning a red-brown; the seeds are glossy and placed along the centre of the legume with a thickened funicle or attachment. This is one of the " Sally's," but goes by the name of " Flax-leaved " or " Green " wattle in this district.

4. *A. decora*, Reichb., or the Handsome Acacia, named from the dense masses of close set racemes on the ends of the

branches, is an insignificant and useless member of the family, only attaining a few feet, and that on the summits of scrubby mountains and in dogwood country. Gladfield, Killarney, Mount Sturt, and the immediate vicinity of Warwick—where it may be seen flowering on the roadside as stunted bushes of three or four feet, are the principal habitats of this form. It very much resembles a small *A. linifolia*, but the phyllodia are scant, slightly larger, and abruptly mucronate by the projection of the single rib ; the gland is also below the middle. The bark is smooth, and often dark coloured on the young branches owing to the presence of a scale insect resembling that infesting the native aurantiaceous plants of this district. The short closely set racemes of dark yellow flower-heads, form dense cylindrical panicles from six inches to a foot in length, with the young leaves projecting beyond ; the flower head is about 4 or 5 lines across with sinuous stamens and square anthers, pollen grains rather larger than those of *A. linifolia*, more irregular in outline, and somewhat quadrangular, the geometric markings clearer and more transparent. I do not fancy this species has been tested as a tannin producer, nor do I think any value could be attached to it. Apart from the fact that it never attains any size, the bark is thin and fibrous ; it is doubtful, even when cut and worked up with the smaller portions of *A. linifolia*, if it would pay, when growing naturally on stony waste land.

5. *A. implexa*, Bentham, is, next to the common " Black Wattle," the species more generally seen at Gladfield, Freestone, Killarney, Canning Downs, in fact, all round Warwick, and is distinguished from *A. longifolia* by its erect and graceful shape, somewhat pendulous and falcate phyllodia and redder bark. It does not seem to have received any separate trivial name, but has been incorporated by non-botanists with all other resembling types as the " Black Wattle." The tree grows, in the scrub soils of Mount Dumaresq, very quickly, those six years old being 30 ft. high and 8 in. through, very erect and tough, retaining the principal trunk to the summit, rarely if ever forking, unless damaged in its young stage. An analysed sample of the bark from New South Wales only yielded 8 per cent. of tannic acid and 20·54 per cent. of extract, while a Queensland specimen

gave double the amount of acid and 33·51 of extract, and that
only from a tree 4 in. in diameter. It also affects Victoria.
In seedlings the first true leaves are bi-pinnate—as in most of
the phyllodinous species—with winged petioles and numerous
pinnæ—up to thirty ; pinnæ oblong, mucronate, and 1-nerved;
young phyllodia often reddish tipped, linear lanceolate and a foot
long. The bark is from a quarter to half an inch thick, fibrous;
when young, red and smooth ; red brown, deeply and irregularly
furrowed, when mature; the sap is very free in October, and the
inner bark sticky and bitter owing to the presence of saponin.
The phyllodia are mostly falcate, 6in. long by $\frac{1}{4}$in. broad,
tapering at both ends, prominently 3-nerved, with numerous
parallel and reticulating veinlets. The flower heads are pale
yellow, globular, about 3 or 4 lines across, few, in loose leafy
panicles 6in. broad and long ; legumes two, four, or six in a
cluster on a common pedicel 1in. long, each 4 to 6 in. long by
3 lines broad, ending in a spur, and contracted, between the
seeds, which are from seven to twelve in number; seeds oval,
$2\frac{1}{2}$ lines by $1\frac{1}{2}$, attached to a white, ultimately coloured funicle,
folded four times at the end of the seed, not passing beneath
or enclosing the seed in any way, and five lines long. In seed
in October at Gladfield, and found in flower and ripe fruit in
January at Killarney and Spring Creek.

6. A. melanoxylon, R. Br. ; literally, the "black wooded"
acacia of the southern colonies of Australia, has extended its
known geographical limit, adding the colony of Queensland to
its list of localities—West Australia being the only one omitted
at the present time. It grows in N.S.W. and Victoria under the
several local names " Blackwood " (the translation of its specific
name), " Lightwood," " Black Sally," " Hickory " and " Silver
Wattle." In Bentham's " Flora Australiensis," ii., 388, it is
thus described—" A small tree, except in Tasmania where it
attains a large size, glabrous, or the young shoots minutely
hoary, the smaller branches angular. False leaves sickle
shaped, oblong, or almost lanceolate, 3 to 4 in. long; in the
common varieties, $\frac{1}{2}$ to 1 in. broad ; obtuse or rarely acute, much
narrowed towards the base, coriaceous, with several longitudinal
nerves, with numerous anastomosing veins. Peduncles 3 or 4
lines long, few together in a short raceme, or sometimes solitary

bearing each a dense globular head of thirty to fifty or more flowers,
mostly 5-merous, and often so closely packed in this head that
the calyces adhere ; calyx more than half as long as the corolla,
thin and shortly toothed. Petals connate above the middle.
Pod elongated, flat, often curved into a circle, 3 or 4 lines broad,
with thickened nerve-like margins. Seeds nearly orbicular,
funicle very long, dilated and coloured from the base, very
flexuose, more or less encircling the seed, in double folds." The
timber of this tree is highly valuable and should not by any
means be sacrificed for the bark, as this can only be classed
amongst those of secondary value for tannin extraction. A
sample of the bark of this tree from the vicinity of Braidwood,
N.S.W., yielded J. H. Maiden 11·12 per cent of tannic acid and
20·63 of extract. This, apparently from an old tree, was of a
dirty brown colour, with white patches, giving the whole a
silvery appearance. It has irregular vertical fissures. and this
circumstance, with the small longitudinal cracks, causes the
outer bark to be rapidly detached in small flakes. The inner
bark or bast is strong and would form an excellent coarse tying
material for local use. (J. H. Maiden in part.)

I found several trees of this species on the top of the Main
Range, between Spicer's Peak and Cunningham's Gap on
January 1st., 1892. The plant from which the specimens were
gathered was situate by the old Ipswich road-side, on the range,
and was a tree between 20 and 30 feet high, spreading, and
having a diameter of 18 in. at 3 feet from the ground. The
bark in every way corresponds with Mr. Maiden's sample as
before described. Not supposing the tree to be any other than
one of the many " black wattles " so common on the range, I
did not gather abundant specimens.

7. *A. longifolia*, Willd. The typical form does not seem to
inhabit the Warwick district, but is represented by the variety
floribunda. It is by far the commonest wattle of the vicinity,
being scattered everywhere, thinly and singly growing to large
trees with a branch spread of thirty to forty feet, and 18 to 24 in.
through the butt. More especially are trees of this size
noticeable on the Killarney and Spring Creek watersheds, in
dense brigalow patches on scrub land, particularly where burnt

off. The general size is, in three or four years, 20 feet high and 4 or 6 in through, and as it suckers from the surface roots very vigorously, soon forms dense plantations in which nothing else can vegetate. The roots are extremely tough and are covered with a yellowish bark, and when cut and brought close to the surface soon push out a crowd of suckers from between the bark and wood at the severed end ; and were they required for propagation this would be a simple and most effective manner of reproduction ; but no one should wish to utilise this variety when A. decurrens or A. pycnantha would thrive in the soil and climate. It is the " Black Wattle " of Queensland often called here " Brigalow." In N.S.W. it receives the names " Golden Wattle," " Hickory " and " White Sallow or Sally " indiscriminately. It is a very secondary tannin producer—a New South Wales specimen only yielding from 2 to 6 per cent. with about 14 per cent. of extract ; the bark is very fibrous and when passed through the mill appears as chopped grass. The other Queensland variety, sophoræ, also yields a small supply of tannic acid, is used in preparing only light skins, and is valued at about 30s. a ton in Queensland. The branches are very slightly flattened, the young shoots reddish, with alternate phyllodia 4-8 in. long, straight or falcate, incurved only at the tip, tapering gradually at both ends. dark green, with a small dark gland near the base on the upper margin. When 4 or 6 in. long they are usually from ½ to over an inch wide. Sometimes, however, on young plants they reach 8 ins. in length and less than ¼in. wide, with three principal nerves and numerous parallel closely branched secondary ones. Flowers yellow on cylindrical spikes, one to three together in the axils of the leaves, forming a somewhat leafy panicle of catkins, each catkin 2 or 3 in. long, and 3 or 4 lines wide ; flowers sessile, 2 or 3 lines long, somewhat interrupted along the rachis which is clothed with minute cellular hairs. Calyx minute, if any; corolla greenish, 4 or 5-lobed, glabrous ; staminal filaments much twisted or straight, covered with papillæ, exserted, about as long again as the corolla, anthers squarish peltate, 2-lobed, 2-celled, laterally splitting and yellow; style twice as long as the filiform stamen, often projecting from one side of the flower ; stigma simple ; and ovary covered with long white hairs. The legumes at first are straight, linear, 3 to 6 in. by 2 or 3 lines, ending in a beak and convex over the seeds, constricted between, then becoming tortuous, until finally they form a curled and matted ball the size of a man's fist, of a red-brown colour, and when freshly split open are a bright yellow inside. The seeds are few for the length of the pod, distant, 2½ lines long, black and shining, and somewhat depressed towards the detached end; attached by a red funicle, thickened into a cup-shaped aril nearly the size of the seed. In flower in March.

The fruit of young trees is often, if not as a rule, abortive, owing to the action of a gall insect, which, laying its eggs in the rachis or common flower stem, causes it to swell to 4 lines thick and fill to repletion with an acrid, bitter sap, probably containing saponin. In a month or so these bodies swell still more, curl up, and assume fantastic more or less globular shapes, 1 to 3 inches across, brittle, and green outside, white within; if opened, numerous circular cavities are noticeable, inhabited by a small white larval which eventually changes into the pupal state, and latterly emerges as an imago—a small wasp-like jet black insect, the male, slender and active, the female extremely obese and rather sluggish. In the early winter months these emerge, and leave the gall dry brown and shrivelled. This gall insect is about 3 lines long when full grown. In the months of August, September, and October the leaves of some of this species are infested with a small golden yellow larva, which eats the outer membranes, causing the leaf to appear flecked as though with a fungoid brand; ultimately this insect turns blackish brown.

8. *A. Cunninghamii*, Hook. This " black wattle," named in honour of the great botanist and explorer, Allan Cunningham, is not at all a common plant on the Gladfield side of Warwick, but is found principally growing on the yellow sandy soil round the hospital and in the Sandy Creek and Rosenthal districts. It seems rather to affect dry aspects in this locality being rarely found in the vicinity of creek banks and swamps as is sometimes the other black wattle, *A. longifolia*. It is a small tree, attaining here the

height of 15 or 20 feet, diameter 4 to 6in., and as a rule
rather sturdy in trunk for its height. The younger branches
are very prominently angular and more or less striate
on the flattened areas. The tips of the young phyllodia
are reddish purple and very tender; mature phyllodia
3 to 5in. long, tapering at both ends, from ¾ to 1½in.
broad in the centre, prominently 3-nerved with multitudinous
secondary parallel nervelets running the full length of the
phyllode often confluent before reaching the petiole proper.
Cylindrical flower spikes axillary, solitary or as many as three or
four together, obliquely erect and straight, 2½ or 3in. long and 4
lines wide ; flower of a bright sulphur ; young buds pyriform,
packed closely to the rachis. If abortive, as often happens in
one crop of bloom of the black wattles, the cluster of spikes hang
to the tree for several weeks and turn a dull red-brown. The
legumes become very flexuose, and are long and narrow, only
about 1½ to 2½ lines broad. In flower in July and August,
fruiting probably in November or December. It is the '' Black
Wattle '' and '' Bastard Myall '' of New South Wales and the '' Black
Wattle '' and Kowarkul of Queensland, the latter a native name.
Dr. T. L. Bancroft says '' This species is the only tanning wattle
which grows near Brisbane in any great abundance.'' A specimen
forwarded by him to Mr. Maiden from Deception Bay gathered
from a tree a foot in diameter gave 12·38 per cent. of acid and
26·95 of extract. The bark is about half an inch thick, under
the outer dark brown scaly portion, and is fibrous within.
I am not aware that it has been utilised at the Warwick tannery,
probably the natural growth is too scarce. Another analysis at
the Indian and Colonial Exhibition, relating to a Queensland
sample, only gives 9 per cent. of tannin and 16·15 per cent. of
extract.

    9. *A. decurrens*, Willd.   The last but decidedly not the least
of the Partial Decade of the Warwick '' wattles.'' This, the well-
known '' Green Wattle '' of Queensland, and supplying the greater
percentage of bark for the purposes of tanning, is commercially the most valuable of '' Acacia '' barks indigenous to this
colony. The dry bark is supposed to fetch a price varying from
£4 to £5 10s. per ton. Tons of this product are transported by
bullock teams to Ipswich from a point on the Main Range

only 25 miles from Warwick. Large tracts of this species may be observed close around the Warwick township, Upper Freestone Creek, portions of Killarney, and scantily at Gladfield, Dalrymple Creek, and in fact in nearly every locality, though the tree is somewhat stunted on the dry sandy ridges. Its usual dimensions here in five or six years' growth are 25 or 30 feet high and 6 to 8in. through. The bark is a vivid green and very smooth, becoming dark and rugged on old boles, and usually very compact, yielding a small degree of fibre. It is the second in quality as a tannin producer, it having yielded from 15 to 36 per cent. of acid and over 60 per cent. extract. These analyses are principally from New South Wales and Victoria bark ; the quality appears to become inferior as we advance northwards, though perhaps the Queensland hot dry-country barks have not been sufficiently tested. The variety here is entirely " mollis "—the A. mollissima of Müeller's " Dichotomous Key." It has been called by the local name " Black Wattle " in New South Wales and often in Victoria and Tasmania ; though usually it passes everywhere under the name of " Green Wattle " or " Silver Wattle." Native names are " Wat-tah," of Cumberland and Camden, New South Wales ; " Garrong," of portions of Victoria, and " Warraworup," of Coranderrk, Victoria. It is widely distributed through the south of South Australia, Tasmania, Victoria, Inner Southern Queensland and most of New South Wales. It has also been known in this locality as the "Golden Wattle," owing probably to the clear yellow tinge assumed by it at a certain season of the year when developing its young shoots. The inflorescence is a very pale yellow, the flower heads globular about 4 lines in diameter. The foliage is exceedingly feathery in appearance ; the leaf varying from 2 in. to 4 in. long and 2 in. or 3 in. broad, with multitudinous leaflets, is endowed with a certain amount of sensitiveness when picked, as in the Mimosæ and the mimosa-leaved Cassia, both common in the district, the latter among the ranges. But so much has been written and said about this species by experts and others who have made a study of it from a commercial point of view, that it would be mere waste of time re-writing anything but that directly concerned with its growth about here. As with the "Black Wattles" this species flowers in favourable seasons twice a year, usually in the midwinter and midsummer months, the ripe seed being obtainable in December and in June or July. The flowering seasons of all Acacias, as also those of the Eucalypts and many other trees in this district, I have observed are very erratic, depending entirely on the preceding rainfall; a tree in full flower in November of a certain year would, probably, on the next anniversary of this event have no flower but nearly ripe fruit and flower buds just showing, I have observed specimens of this species under notice, in full flower in January on the banks of the Condamine River, while shrubs close at hand (of the same) were laden with ripening legumes.

NOTES ON TWO SPECIES OF PEZIZA.

BY

C. Julian Gwyther.

(Read on 7th December, 1893).

In the warm damp months of autumn, at Gladfield, Warwick, especially during August and September, the ordinary "cow-droppings" which have been exposed to wind and rain assume a yellowish tinge when viewed from a distance, and on closer examination are seen to be infested with examples of a minute yellow cup-shaped—or rather saucer-shaped—fungus which in a few days spreads from an individually almost invisible plant to one about $1\frac{1}{2}$ lines in diameter. The second species of the same genus of fungi may not be noticed until one examines the mound minutely. This is of a brown wine-colour and grows much larger, i.e., to 3 lines in width. At times both forms may be seen crowded together on the self-same "dropping," and on other occasions one may have to search diligently to find any specimens of the brown species at all, for this is by far the rarest of the two. The yellow species is very common, scarcely a mound but that supports several thousands. The droppings of cattle almost exclusively yield these forms, and rarely if ever are they to be seen on those of horses.

No. 1 is smooth and yellow to 1½ lines across, slightly saucer-shaped or plane above and thick and fleshy below, as deep as it is wide, usually very regular as to outline, being generally quite circular. When sliced, and a section placed beneath a quarter inch objective, it will be observed to be composed of numerous asci or partially oblong sacs, usually very regularly disposed, each containing eight oblong or oval spores, uniseriate and regular, or somewhat confused in arrangement and partially bi-seriate, interspersed very sparsely with 8 jointed very small and transparent rods named paraphyses.

No. 2 is of a fleshy, wine-coloured brown, to 3½ lines across, slightly cup-shaped, though plane above and convex below, with a short distinct stem-root. It eventually dries dark brown, curling at the margins—which become crimped and whitish-gray. The plants of this species grow, in some cases, so closely together as to become angular by mutual pressure. The contents are gelatinous, greenish-yellow and large, composed of 8-spored asci. These are transparent, club-shaped, and perforated at the apex when mature for the exit of the spores. These latter are smooth, oval, transparent, and packed obliquely or in a confused manner. At the bases of the asci may be observed the numerous paraphyses or sterile asci, somewhat short and one-celled only. These attain about half the length of the ascus or spore-sac. These species of Peziza never germinate on the mounds until the more offensive organic matters composing the substance they affect have been thoroughly washed out by rain. The collector, therefore, need be in no fear of defiling himself in securing examples of either.

The drawings illustrating these fungi and their microscopical structure which are submitted for the inspection of the members of the Society will serve to illustrate my statements.

A RARE WARWICK ORCHID, ACIANTHUS FORNICATUS.

BY

C. Julian Gwyther.

(Read on 1st February, 1894).

[This paper related to a terrestrial orchid bearing the above name, which had been found by the author, during April and May of the preceding year, flowering on the dry stony ridges of Charley's Gully, a locality situated on the watershed between Upper Freestone and Glengallan creeks. Here it occurred gregariously, occupying an area of about two square chains, attaining a height of from six to fifteen inches. Notwithstanding the fact of the Warwick District having been carefully explored by the author during many months for the purpose of elucidating its flora, this little plant had been met with nowhere else than at the above-mentioned spot. The paper also comprised a very full description of the orchid itself and the principal structural features alluded to were further illustrated by carefully executed drawings. Acianthus fornicatus has been previously dealt with from the point of view taken by the author by other writers on Australian botany, and therefore his Note is passed over, this reference only being made to its subject matter.—Ed.]

THE INSECT ENEMIES OF CEREALS BELONGING TO THE GENUS CECIDOMYIA.

BY

HENRY TRYON.

(Read on 5th April, 1894).

The Hessian fly (Diplosis destructor), its nature and mode of injury, and the history of its occurrence and extent of its ravages on the Continent of Europe, in the United States, in Great Britain, and in New Zealand, were first dealt with ; and then the wheat midges (Diplosis tritici and D. aurantiaca) and other destructive species were similarly treated of.

These insects might, it was said, be regarded as forming two groups, the first containing the Hessian fly—the tiny maggots of which injured the stems of wheat in the regions of the joints ; and the second, including Diplosis tritici and its associate, which confined their attention to its florets, and consequently rendered them infertile. As a representative of the first of these divisions, Mr. Tryon exhibited a sample of the celebrated blue grass (Andropogon sericeus), regarded as being one of the best fodder-grasses in Australia, every stalk of which had one or more enlongated swellings at the joints, and so was materially damaged. These galls had been occasioned by the grubs of a minute gnat-like insect—Lasioptera vastatrix—specimens of which were passed around. This was the only cecidomyid which had hitherto been shown to be destructive to vegetation in Australia, Mr. F. A. A. Skuse, its describer, having reported that it was very injurious to fodder in the Parkes District of New South Wales, where alone it had been previously met with. This pest, it was remarked, is quite common in Brisbane and its vicinity, and doubtless does considerable harm.

To explain the action of the wheat midge, Mr. Tryon further exhibited a second species of Diplosis, which he had lately found damaging the inflorescence of the broom sorghum.

G

The following facts concerning the life history of this pest had, amongst others, he added, been already elicited. The parent insect, which is a minute red-bodied gnat-like fly, whose body measures approximately but $1\frac{1}{3}$ line in length, and which has a wing expansion of $1\frac{1}{2}$ line, alights upon one of the florets of the spikelet of the broom sorghum about the time of its first opening and before the anthers have shed their pollen and by means of a needle-like retractile organ—the ovipositor, which equals its body in length, deposits one egg or more in contact with the essential organs of the flower, the perfect florets being alone selected for this purpose. Each female insect lays from seventy to eighty eggs. These, which are invisible to the naked eye, are orange-red in colour. They are cylindrical in form, but unlike what has been observed in other related insects, are drawn out to a long blunt point at one extremity, a feature which doubtless secures them from being blown from their resting place. The tiny maggots when hatched feed upon the ovary of the flower and hinder its further development, so that the formation of seed is altogether checked. They are about $\frac{2}{3}$ line in length when extended, and like the eggs orange-red in colour. They continue to derive nutriment from the flower until the seed which is free from their attack is ripe and harvested, and even then many have not yet passed into the pupa or chrysalis condition. These final transformations are undergone within the dead and often fungus-infested floret; though the maggot has occasionally passed previously to the narrow space which intervenes between the flowering and empty glume. Some it is thought may drop to the ground and transform therein. It being impracticable to husk either broom sorghum seed or that of other sorghums, the pest may be easily conveyed from one district to another. Already this insect, confined as far as is at present known to Southern Queensland, and believed to be a native species, is extensively parasitised by a minute hymenopterous fly belonging to the family Chalcidæ, which closely resembles the parasite which Mr. Enoch has lately sent from England to the United States, and also to New Zealand, to assist in lessening the depredations of the Hessian fly in these regions. Should the present cecidomyid transfer its attention to the florets of other cereals, such as those of the wheat, or should the wheat midge become established in Australia, this parasite will be available for a similar purpose to that subserved by the Semiotellus nigripes, as above mentioned, in the case of the Hessian fly. The observations which led to the discovery of this broom sorghum cecidomyid were prompted, it was added, by our Agricultural Department, and to it, therefore, the Society was accordingly in-indebted.

As a further instance of this class of insect pests Mr. Tryon exhibited a cecidomyid from Alternanthera versicolor—a favourite plant for carpet work and borders of gardens.— *Abstract.*

PRESIDENTIAL ADDRESS, 1893.

BY

HENRY TRYON.

(Read on 19th April, 1894).

[This address had for its subject " A New Potato Disease," and related to a malady, originated by bacteria, affecting this esculent in the Ravensbourne, Corinda, and other districts of Southern Queensland. The same theme formed the subject of a Special Report to the Department of Agriculture of Queensland, and is alluded to in the Annual Report, 1893-4, of that institution.—ED.]

NOTES ON RECENT ACQUISITIONS—LEPIDOPTERA.

BY

R. ILLIDGE.

(Read on 7th June, 1894.)

These comprised descriptions of the metamorphoses and habits of a number of very beautiful local butterflies and moths, which were passed around for inspection. Amongst the former insects were two strangely different butterflies, one almost black with cream-coloured markings, and the other tawny yellow. These were both named Heteronympha mirifica, *Butler*, and were said to be examples of a satyrid butterfly scarce about Brisbane, and confined to dense scrubs. The male had long been thought to belong to a different species from its consort, and been accordingly named in 1875, by Mr. W. H. Miskin, after the late Mr. Sylvester Diggles. Another butterfly was the lycænid Holochila Heathii, *Cox*, which was remarked as being also rare about Brisbane, being apparently confined to the hills. The most noteworthy insect shown was, however, one of the largest and handsomest of the Hesperidæ or Skippers—Netrocoryne or Casyapa beata. Of this Mr. Illidge remarks as follows :—" This skipper is only equalled in size amongst the Australian species of skippers, and surpassed in beauty by Euschemon Rafflesiæ. The caterpillar and chrysalis of the rare insect are now for the first time exhibited. It is by no means voracious, and a tree might be covered with it and yet reveal no signs of its presence save for the occurrence of leaves here and there in pairs connected together by silken threads. Though the caterpillar shown is feeding upon the camphor laurel, I have lately ascertained that its proper food-plants are Tristania conferta and one of the scrub Laurineæ." Amongst the moths were Panacra lignaria and P. Joanna, two hawk-moths which were especially noteworthy for their rarity. Somewhat resembling huge bees, were examples of another member of the Sphingidæ named Sesia

Kingii. " The caterpillar of this hawk-moth," it was remarked,
" is a conspicuous object at times on our Gardenias, and being
usually of a dark fuscous colour harmonises well with that of the
stems. It is, however, occasionally green, with the same special
markings as when of a darker hue. This moth is noteworthy on
account of the wings being for the greater part covered with
golden-ochreous scales, which are so loosely attached that one
has merely to blow upon them and they will begin to disappear,
and it is only therefore by rearing the insect in confinement
that absolutely perfect examples can be secured." Several
interesting geometer moths were alluded to in the paper,
amongst them being the large silky-white Thalaina punctilinea
from the southern colonies, several different varieties of
Monoctenia, including a new species of the genus reared from
caterpillars feeding upon the silky oak (Grevillea robusta), and
resembling one form of M. vinaria. Of other geometrid moths
remarkable for their bright-green prevalent colours, Mr. Illidge
stated as follows :—" Iodis metaspila has a caterpillar which has
curious side projections, causing it to look somewhat like a bit
of jagged and broken leaf, in which respect it so closely resembles
the caterpillar of a congener, 1. picroides, and when side by side
one could not separate the two species. Iodis partita is another
beautiful species, the caterpillar of which has lately come under
observation. It exhibits also the side projections ; but has,
further, the curious habit of attracting pieces of leaves and
flowers to these appendages. Iodis mariæ, *Lucas*, a third species
of the genus, presents us with a caterpillar still more singular, it
being completely hidden under a mantle composed of pieces of
leaves and blossoms." Other moths noticed were the large
yellow and dark gray Danima banksiæ, whose large and
handsome sphinx-like caterpillar fed voraciously on Banksia,
Grevillea, and other proteaceous trees ; the water-marked, white,
silk-like Porthesia collucens of Dr. Lucas, a rarity, whose
capture was amusingly described ; and Asura cervicalis, a
lithosid, whose dark hairy caterpillar feeds upon the camphor
laurel. Several moths having wood-feeding larvæ, and belonging
to the genus Cryptophaga, were also commented upon in the
paper and likewise exhibited.—ED.

BEAN AND PEA WEEVILS.

BY

HENRY TRYON.

(Read on 9th July, 1894).

AMONGST the insects ordinarily known as weevils is a group composed of stoutly built beetles which have the snout, so conspicuous an object in the common grain weevil, scarcely if at all developed. These weevils, of which upwards of 400 different species have been described, and which are technically designated the Bruchidæ, feed and undergo their transformations within the pods and fruit capsules of various plants, the beans, peas, pulses, and leguminosæ generally being specially affected by them, though they also occur in the fruits of the Hibiscus of the Ipomœa, &c., being especially destructive to the seeds which these organs contain. As a rule the members of each species confine their attention to the seeds of a single kind of plant, but some on the other hand have a fairly extensive dietary.

Mr. G. Masters, in his well-known Catalogue of Australian Coleoptera, published in 1886, includes but a single species of Bruchus therein. There is evidence, however, forthcoming to prove that the family Bruchidæ is by no means so scantily represented here, and of those members occurring at Brisbane alone there are at least three—each of extreme economic importance—which now have an Australian habitat assigned to them for the first time. These, it may be, however, remarked, are all introduced insects, and two, it is feared, have come to stay, and are really established in the colony.

The Bean Weevil.—First there is the bean weevil. Bruchus obtectus, Say, or as it is better known Bruchus fabæ, of Fitch, Riley, and other writers. This is an ashy brown coloured beetle, measuring from 13/100th to 15/100th of an inch in length, with slight indications of alternating whitish and dusky lines on its wing-covers, and the feelers or antennæ parti-coloured

—these organs having the four basal and terminal joints yellow.
It is the habit of the insect referred to to alight upon the green
pod of the growing bean plant and after gnawing a tiny slit
along the suture, should an opening not naturally occur there,
to deposit—by means of a curved telescopic ovipositor—little
groups of eggs near the point of attachment of one or more of
the contained seeds. Shortly after this event the beetle itself
dies. On hatching out the grubs, which are at this time of
microscopic dimensions, penetrate the beans proper and feeding
within the latter are harvested together with the seeds that they
infest, their detection then being a matter of no little difficulty.
Several individuals usually occur at one time within each seed
thus affected. After awhile the beans attacked present small
translucent areas on their surface, as if their skins at these
points had been partly permeated by grease. These places
mark the position of the more superficial burrowings. Some,
however, of these marks are quite circular in outline, and their
special form is thus accounted for. When the grub is full fed it
gnaws a cylindrical tunnel outwards, and this ends immediately
at the skin of the seed, this even being partly cut through in a
circular manner. The grub then makes a cell just within this
outer boundary of its tunnel, and undergoes its further transformations therein. Eventually it pushes outwards the small disc
which confined it, and emerging as a perfect beetle leaves in the
bean a cleanly cut hole to mark the event. If meanwhile the
bean has been planted the Bruchus weevil comes forth from the
ground, and can sustain itself for a month or more on the tissue
of the young plant, or by occasional visits to the blossoms of
neighbouring flowers ; until opportunity for laying its eggs, as
previously described, has arisen. Should the bean, on the other
hand, remain in the store the beetle fastens its eggs to the
outside of it, using for the purpose a sticky material which
quickly hardens on exposure, and the grubs on issuing penetrate
the skin and feed therein. Generation after generation may
thus arise and be supported, and so the insect multiplies. It is
stated that no bean is proof against the attack of this insect. In
Brisbane it has been noticed by me infesting the Madagascar,
the ordinary white haricot bean, and a small pale dun French
bean. In the case of a sample of the first mentioned procured

in Brisbane less than 10 per cent. of the beans were free from injury from this cause. When again the damaged beans are planted the effects due to the injury occasioned by the bean weevil are very manifest, for—as has been recorded by Professor E. A. Popenoe—as the outcome of investigations conducted at the Kansas State Experiment Station with numerous varieties of these esculents, but 30 per cent. can survive the germinating stage, and of this amount but few individual plants make further growth owing to the more or less extensive damage which the seed leaves have experienced. The history of our knowledge of this pest, which is very significant, may be briefly referred to. It is usually regarded as being a native of North America. In 1831, in which year it was first described by Say, it was noticed as being associated with an indigenous American plant belonging to the genus Astralagus, but not until 1860, or until the lapse of nearly thirty years, did it earn notoriety by becoming a destroyer of cultivated beans. Within ten years, however, of the latter event it had become widely dispersed, and had displayed its harmful propensities in nearly every State of the American Union, and soon travelled even beyond the limits of the New World, for in 1875 it was even reintroduced to America in beans displayed at the Philadelphia International Exhibition from several foreign countries. The fact of the possibility—already adverted to—of its increase within stored beans favours its journeying to all countries which are even indirectly commercially related to its original home. And thus it is not surprising that it is now reported as existing in the West Indies, South Africa, Madeira, the Canaries, the Mediterranean basin, Persia, and finally Australia. How long it has existed here is uncertain, but it was first noticed by me in Brisbane four years since infesting haricot beans, and is already reported to be here in the bean crop when this is harvested.

The Larger Pea Weevil.—The second of these insects to be dealt with is apparently the notorious pea weevil, Bruchus pisorum, described by Linnæus in 1756. This Bruchus is rather larger than the preceding species, and is also a much more gaily hued insect, its prevailing colours being rusty red and black. It also has a conspicuous white spot on the thorax behind, and two large black blotches on the exposed portion of the hind-body immediately behind the wing-covers—features not present in the bean weevil. As in the case of the latter insect, Bruchus pisorum attacks its food plant when this is still growing and when the pods are green, but long before they are fully developed, the egg being deposited superficially on the sides of the legume, and the tiny grub on hatching out mining its way inwards until the seed is reached. Unlike what occurs in the case of the bean weevil, but a single grub occurs in each pea. In other respects, however, the life histories of the two insects are somewhat similar. Bruchus pisorum is of European origin, and from the Mediterranean area has been spread widely by commerce, having long since proved a very serious pest in the fields and gardens of the United States. The specimens exhibited were found on cow peas from the northern part of Queensland, and afford the only instance as yet known to me of the occurrence of this insect in the colony, though this pea weevil is suspected as having occasioned the entire destruction of a parcel of these legumes received at Bingera Plantation from Brisbane, as reported to the writer by Mr. W. Gibson, one of the proprietors.

The Smaller Pea Weevil.—The third member of the Bruchidæ to be noticed on this occasion as occurring here is Bruchus chinensis. This is very distinct in appearance from the two weevils previously referred to—scarcely exceeding half the size of either. It, however, somewhat resembles the pea weevil in colouration, being ferruginous and black, but there is more white upon the wing-covers. It moreover lacks the two dark blotches on the hind-body above, but this in B. chinensis is traversed by a longitudinal white line. The sexes again in the present pea weevil are not alike, but differ one from the other both in structure and colour. In one the feelers or antennæ are conspicuously branched, whereas its consort not only lacks this feature but has a much paler livery—the black being largely replaced by reddish brown. The habits of this insect are doubtless very similar to those of its congeners, it occurring not only in the store but also in the field ; and as in the case of the bean weevil several larvæ are often met with in the same seed. Like the two preceding weevils it is now almost a cosmopolitan insect, being introduced with seed into one country after another. It was described by Fabricius as a European insect quite a hundred

years since. It feeds on the seeds of several different Leguminosæ, having been reported as infesting the grams, pigeon peas
(Cajanus indicus), Chinese beans, &c. The examples on exhibition were procured in a parcel of seed of the sugar pea directly
imported from Germany and in two or three varieties of cow
peas from the northern part of this colony. Mr. C. J. Wild,
when at Kamerunga in 1890, found there examples of a Bruchus,
which are evidently referable to the species under notice,
inhabiting the seed pods of a native tree, and thus there is
evidence of its having already become naturalised in the colony.

In conclusion it may be urged that the means which are
available for staying the increase of these bean and pea weevils
would if generally enforced now, be attended by far-reaching
beneficial results.

HEXABRANCHUS FLAMMULATUS, *Q. & G.*

BY

C. J. WILD, F.L.S.

(Read on 19th July, 1894).

This is a large shell-less mollusc, and one of the living
treasures of the deep obtained by a member of the famous
schnapper fishing party which visited the Tweed Heads near our
southern border on Saturday, 14th July. It is a most strikingly
beautiful object of its kind. It measures no less than 7½ inches
in length, is somewhat flattened, and of a broadly oval outline.
Its general colour is coral red, and it is to a large extent translucent. The body on all sides is outwardly suddenly compressed,
passing into a thin, broad, elegantly-frilled border. The frill
thus formed, is of a deep uniform red colour and is narrowly
edged with pale violet and when extended it gives the body an
extreme breadth of quite 6 inches. The slightly convex back is
perfectly smooth, and as the red coloration in this position takes
the form of an exceedingly fine network which permits the pale
epidermis to be seen through, this part appears of a paler hue
than the encircling frill. In front, on either side of the middle

line, is a deep red, club-like, protuberant body, the tentacle; whilst towards the hind border, disposed in a wide circle around a raised orifice, is a series of eight erect, pale brown objects resembling miniature trees. These have their main stem and branches pure white with an axial red line along all the ramifications. These organs are the branchiæ and subserve the purpose of respiration. The under surface of the body is occupied by a broad, light red, muscular foot, and this has the margin here and there puckered, and is rounded at both ends; it extends somewhat beyond the body proper behind. Outside the edge of this foot the frill beneath is sprinkled with minute dots of red, which, being here and there more densely distributed, present a clouded appearance. Beyond the front border of the foot nestled the bluntly-conical head, almost wholly occupied beneath by two large, red, thick, leaf-like bodies—the labiæ, or lips—which spring horizontally one on either side from a conspicuous mouth. Creeping slowly along the rocky sea bottom in and out amongst numerous zoophytes, with its delicate frill waving and trembling with every motion of the surrounding tide, this object would appear a thing of beauty not soon to be forgotten, and though to all appearances a *bonne bouche* for a voracious schnapper or parrot-fish, yet secure probably from their attack through being rendered distasteful by a mucous secretion—noisome, no doubt, as in the case of that poured forth by the allied nudibranch mollusc, Aplysia, with which in these seas Hexabranchus is associated.

The genus Hexabranchus has recently been dealt with by Dr. Rudolf Bergh in an article entitled "Nudibranchien von Meere der Insel Mauritius" contained in Dr. C. Semper's well-known "Reisen in Archipel der Phillipinen" (Wiesenbaden, 1878-1889). From this memoir it would appear that the previously characterised species are now restricted to eight individual forms exhibiting great variation and that even one of these eight is of doubtful validity. Also that the individual above described and on exhibition, is evidently an example of Hexabranchus flammulatus of Mons. Quoy and Gaimard ("Voyage de l'Astrolabe II," 1832, p. 257, pl. 17, figs. 6-8), figured and described by these naturalists under the name given, and also by Souleyet under the designation Hexabranchus sandwichensis in his "Voyage de la Bonite" (Zoologie II, 1852).

CONFECTIONERY PESTS.

BY

C. J. WILD, F.L.S.

(Read on 4th October, 1894).

[This related to the beetles Rhizopertha pusilla and
Sylvanus surinamensis found infesting different forms of
chocolate met with in Brisbane in confectioners' trade samples.
—Ed.]

THE DATE PALM FOR QUEENSLAND. *

BY

T. Morris Macknight, F.L.S.

(Read on November 1st, 1894).

The Date Palm is an example of extraordinary fruitfulness.
Next to the cocoanut it is unquestionably the most interesting
and useful of the palm tribe. Without it the desert would be
uninhabitable. Do we not understand, then, the gratefulness
of the Arab towards a tree which can derive its nourishment
from the scorching sand, the scarcely less burning airs of
heaven, and the brackish waters beneath the soil, which are fatal
to all other kinds of vegetation ; which retains its verdure fresh
in the glare of a pitiless sun ; which provides him with beams
and coverings for his tent ; cordage for the harness of his horses
and mules ; fruit to satisfy his hunger ? What the vine is to
the Italian, the cocoanut tree to the Polynesian, the Date
Palm is to the Arab. And more—far more. This single tree has
peopled the desert. Without it the tribes of the Sahara would
cease to be. The wealth of an oasis is computed by the number
of its date trees.

---

* The author prefaced his paper with the statement that he made no pretence of
having an expert knowledge of his subject. He had collected information from all the
sources which were available to him, and had given the matter his consideration for
some time past. The results of this compilation he submitted as a guide to those in
search of summary on the subject.

HABITAT.

The habitat of the date is North Africa, Arabia, Persia, Egypt, Nubia, Syria, and it does not go further east than the mouth of the Indus. It is indigenous in the Canary Isles ; wanting in the south of Senegal, and it no longer appears in the Oasis of Darfur, between the 13deg. and 15deg. of lat. The zone in which it grows well in general is that between 35deg. and 19deg. north. According to Link (Die Urwelt., I., p. 347), it flowers freely in the south of Europe, as in Sicily, the Morea, and the south of Spain ; and also bears fruit there, though this is not sweet. In Sicily it still grows at 1700ft.—namely at Aderno and Trecastagne on Etna, but it probably does not bear fruit on this island—(Philippi on Vegetation of Etna, "Linnæa," vol. 7, p. 731). It needs 5100deg. F. of heat accumulated during eight months for the date to ripen its fruit perfectly. If the sum of the heat be less the fruits set, but they do not grow to their full dimensions ; they also remain bitter to the taste, and lack much of the sugar and albumen, to which they owe their nutritive properties. The requisite conditions are realised in the Sahara. The mean temperature of the year there averages from 68deg. to 76deg., according to the locality. The heat commences in April, and does not cease till October. Keith Johnston's "Physical Atlas" gives the temperature in summer and winter as—July, 81deg. to 86deg. ; January, 52deg. to 61deg. ; mean temperature (annual), 68deg. to 76deg. Biskra, the celebrated date-growing district in North Africa, is in lat. 34deg. 51min., altitude 410ft. ; it faces towards the hot tropical south, and is protected by mountains on the north side. It has an annual mean temperature of 68·5deg. (January 50·2deg., July, 89·8deg.) The thermometer seldom sinks in the cold season more than 2deg. below freezing point, and the date can endure 6deg. of frost.

The neighbourhood of the sea is unfavourable to the production of good dates. The general altitude of the central districts of North Africa, where it thrives, is 600ft. to 2000ft. ; the Date Palm also grows in some Egyptian oases from sea level to 600ft. The lower portions of the rivers Euphrates and Tigris in Turkey are from sea level to 600ft.

The amount of annual rainfall requisite for the best dates is from 5in. to 10in. ; for those of inferior qualities from 10in. to

25in. Mr. A. S. White, secretary of the Royal Geographical
Society of Scotland, gives, in his work, the " Development of
Africa," 1890, a map of the rainfalls in North Africa, Arabia,
and Persia, which may be profitably referred to in this connection. Although the date requires a hot, dry climate, yet its
roots must have access to moisture. And though it is essentially
a tree belonging to desert regions, yet it is confined to the oases
in the these deserts where water is found. It flourishes in rain-
less countries, but only where there is moisture in the soil,
either naturally or produced by irrigation.

IRRIGATION AND OASES.

The " Oases of the Tableland," writes Charles Martins in
his ' Du Spitzberg au Sahara,' " are each watered by a stream
or copious spring, and are but a short distance from the Mediterranean region. The oasis of El Kantara is the first (Mangin)
we met on leaving the Mediterranean region to penetrate to the
Sahara through a ravine called ' The Mouth of the Desert.' It
is 1800ft. above sea level, and its temperature just suffices to
enable the dates to ripen. The oases of the Valleys of Erosion
are watered by natural or artesian wells. An example is Ouargla,
situated in a profound hollow. The palms are planted at the
rate of 1000 to 1100 a hectare (two acres). Outside the gardens
grow some wild date palms, which yield a smaller crop, but
whose fruit is much more savoury. The Oases of the Sandy
Desert need water. The trees are here planted in conical cavities
hollowed by the hand of man, that their roots may strike down
to the subterranean reservoir which is to nourish them. These
cavities are 18ft., 25ft., or 30ft. deep. The slopes around these
hollow gardens are stayed indifferently well by a matting of palm
leaves. The wells are in the centre, and not deeper than 25ft.
These oases have a very precarious existence, as a gust of wind
may bury them under an avalanche of sand. Every oasis is
composed, in the main, of palms, which seem to form a continuous forest ; but in reality they are planted in rows and in
gardens separated from one another by walls of earth, which
are pierced with an aperture to admit of the entrance of the
irrigating rill into the enclosed square. The soil employed in
the construction of the walls is removed from the paths, which

are consequently below the surface, and can be employed for a double purpose : they facilitate circulation in the oasis, and the waters, after having refreshed the gardens, discharge themselves into these hollow ways."

SOIL.

Meyen, in his " Geography of Plants," page 2, states that a sandy soil suits the date best; and Sonnini in his " Travels in Egypt" saw it growing in the sands as well as in the more fertile parts.   It will luxuriate even in saltish soil, and the water for its irrigation may be slightly brackish.   The artesian water of the Oued Rir district in Algeria contains from 0·57 oz. to 1·07 oz. of dry salt in a gallon.   Brigade-surgeon Bonavia says that on the whole it thrives best in sandy, granitic, schistic, and calcareous soils.   The northern half of Arabia, which is an important centre for date culture, is granitic.

INFLORESCENCE.

The date is a diœcious tree, having the male flowers on one plant, and the female or fruiting ones on another.   The male flowers are considerably larger than the female, furnished with stamens only, and form a closed-up, folded, grape-like ball (previous to the ripening of the pollen) in an envelope called the spathe.   " It blossoms," says Mr. Tristram in his book ' The Great Sahara,' " in the month of March.   The male flower is borne on a very short calyx, a thin petalous corolla much larger, with six stamens, furnished with long linear anthers, the two cells of which open themselves from within by two longitudinal slits.   The female flowers present a double floral envelope, each whorl of which is formed of three pieces, constituting three distinct pistils, each surmounted by a stigma in the form of a hook.   Of these three pistils one only develops itself, ripens, and becomes an elongated ovoid berry, with a slight epidermis of a yellowish red, a solid and slightly viscous pulp, and an endocarp represented by a slight pellicle enveloping the nucleus, which is the seed.   The seed is grooved, and on the opposite side of it is a depression containing the germ."   Baron Mueller states that one male tree is considered sufficient for fifty females. Watts allows one or two males to ʲfrom eighty to two hundred trees.

PROPAGATION.

The best trees are produced from suckers from three to four years old, having an average weight of about 6lb. Those raised from seed are much slower in maturing, and are generally poor. The sucker is taken from the foot of the stem of an adult tree; when first planted it must be watered daily for six weeks, and on alternate days for another six weeks, after which the trees are watered once a week in summer, and every month in winter. The nut does not commence to germinate until from six to twelve months after planting have elapsed, and grows very slowly for the first two years. The trees yield fruit in from five to six years, and are in full bearing at from twenty to twenty-five years, after which they continue fruitful for about 150 years. Several bunches of flowers are formed in a season, each producing often as many as 200 dates. Select trees are recorded as having borne a crop worth £2, but the average may be put down at 4s. per tree annually, common kinds less than 1s. A good date tree is sometimes exchanged for a camel in North Africa.

FECUNDATION.

"In Algeria and all over the East." says M. Cossona, a botanist who has studied the subject on the spot. "towards the month of April the tree begins to flower, and then artificial fecundation is practised extensively. The male spathes are opened at the time when a sort of crackling is produced under the finger, which indicates that the pollen of the flowers in the cluster is sufficiently developed. yet has not escaped from the anthers; the cluster is then divided into portions, each containing seven, or eight, blooms. Having placed these pieces in the hood of his burnous, the workman climbs to the summit of the female tree, supporting himself by a loop of cord passed round his loins, and at the same time round the trunk of the tree, and, having split open the spathe with a knife, he slips in one of the fragments, which he interlaces with the branches of the female cluster, the fecundation of which is made certain." Archer says that wild plants are fecundated by bees. The Arabs even keep the pollen from one year to another in case the male flower should fail the succeeding season. According to Watts the pollen is said to remain active for one or two months after its removal from the tree, so the flower is carefully kept and used as occasion demands. Hasselquist, who travelled in Egypt, describes the operation as follows:—" When the spadix has female flowers that come out of its spathe, they search on a tree that has male flowers, which they know by experience, for the spadix has not yet burst out of its spathe. This they open, take out the spadix, and cut it lengthwise in several pieces, but take care not to hurt the flowers. A piece of this spadix, with male flowers, they put lengthwise between the small branches of the spadix which has female flowers, and then lay the leaf of a palm over the branches. In this situation I yet saw the greatest part of the spadices which bore their young fruit; but the male flowers which were put between were withered. The Arab also stated that unless they in this manner wed and fecundate the date tree it bears no fruit; secondly, they always take the precaution to preserve some unopened spathe, with male flowers, from one year to another, to be applied for this purpose in case the male flowers should miscarry or suffer damage : thirdly, if they permit the spadix of the male flowers to burst or come out it becomes useless for fecundation ; therefore the person who cultivates date trees must be careful to hit the right time of assisting the fecundation, which is almost the only nicety in their cultivation."

To climb trees which have no branches but at the top, and the straight and slender stem, of which cannot support a ladder, the Egyptians employ a sort of girth fastened to a rope, that they pass round the tree. On this girth they seat themselves and rest their weight ; then, with the assistance of their feet, and holding the cord in both hands, they contrive to force the noose suddenly upwards so as to catch the rugged protuberances with which the stem is symmetrically studded, formed at the origin of the branch-like leaves, that are annually cut. By means of these successive springs the top of the tree is reached, where, still sitting, they work at their ease, either in lopping off the leaves or gathering fruit, and afterwards descend in the same manner.

Professor Burnett says the age of bearing is from six to ten years. Haldane says seven years. Baron Mueller says that trees from suckers commence to bear in five years and are in full bearing in ten years.

H

The fig, pomegranate, and apricot, and sometimes the olive, are grown as auxiliary crops. I would suggest also the water melon, pumpkin, vegetable marrow, and lucerne.

VARIETIES.

Dr. James Richardson in a letter in "Hooker's Journal of Botany," Vol. II, writing of the dates of Fezzan, describes forty-six varieties. Nineteen-twentieths of the inhabitants of Fezzan during nine months of the year live on dates. In Northern Arabia there are more than a hundred kinds of dates, each of which is peculiar to a district, and has its own special virtues. Many varieties of dates exist, differing in shape, size, and colour of the fruit. Those of Gomera are large, and contain no seed. The Zadie variety produces the heaviest crop, averaging in full bearing trees 300lbs. to the tree. Professor Naudin states that the variety Datheres-sifia ripens its fruit early in the season. The Deglet nour is considered the best for keeping.

TREATMENT OF FRUITS.

Four or five months after the operation of fecundation has been performed the dates begin to swell, and when they have attained nearly their full size (about the beginning of August) they are carefully tied to the base of the leaves to prevent them from being beaten and bruised by the wind. If meant to be preserved they are gathered a little before they are ripe, but when they are intended to be eaten fresh they are allowed to ripen perfectly, in which state they are very agreeable and refreshing. Ripe dates cannot be kept any length of time or conveyed to any very great distance without fermenting and becoming acid, and therefore those whith are intended for storing up or for being carried to a distant market are dried in the sun on mats. They are sent in this way to Europe from the Levant and Barbary. Each tree is capable of yielding only a certain number of good fruits, and on adult trees not more than twelve bunches are left to ripen. The whole cluster of fruit is cut before it is quite ripe, when it is put into a basket made for the purpose, having no other opening than a hole through which the branching extremity of the cluster projects. In this situation the dates ripen successively.

In the Hedjaz (which is the northern half of Arabia) the new fruit, called *ruteb*, comes in at the end of June and lasts two months. The people cannot therefore depend on the new fruit alone, but during the ten months of the year when no ripe dates can be procured principally subsist on date paste, called *adjoue*, which is prepared by pressing the fruit, when fully matured, into large baskets. "When the dates are allowed to remain on the tree till they are quite ripe, and have become soft and of a high red colour, they are formed into a hard solid paste or cake called *adjoue*. This is obtained by pressing the ripe dates forcibly into large baskets, each containing about 2cwt. In this state," continues Burckhardt, "the Bedouins export the *adjoue*, and in the market it is cut out of the basket and sold by the pound. During the monsoon the ships from the Persian Gulf bring *adjoue* from Bussorah to Djidda for sale in small baskets weighing about 10lb. each ; this kind is preferred to every other."

The date seeds or kernels are soaked for two days in water, when they become softened, and are given to camels, cows, and sheep instead of barley. There are shops in Medina, in Arabia, where nothing else is sold except date kernels, and the beggars are continually employed in all the main streets in picking up those that are thrown away.

The best fruit is that which is gathered just before it is ripe and is exposed to the sun for several days to mature. The crushed dates which arrive in England in bulk are inferior and damaged, having ripened on the trees and fallen. I have seen some beautiful dates in London on the stalks. These in the same way as raisins, have the short pedicels left on them. Then, again, I have seen in Port Said dates, prepared somewhat as we often see them in shops in Brisbane, sold very cheaply, being, I suppose, the refuse of the date groves pressed into a paste or soft mass. This is sold by weight in chunks. In Egypt, the dates of Upper Egypt and the Oases are those which are the most delicate. The hotter and drier the climate the richer is the date, and near the coast the poor fruit is fit only for animals, as mentioned in "French Colonies," by Bonwick, 1886.

Miscellaneous.

Tunis has 2,000,000 date trees; Egypt, 4,000,000; Bussorah, in Turkey, has enormous date groves stretching along both banks of the Euphrates for a distance of over 140 miles, yielding 40,000 tons in good seasons.

The price in England in March, 1894, was—Bussorah, (boxes), 9s. to 13s. 8d. per cwt. ; Tafilet, 44s. to 50s. per cwt.

Dates contain more than half their weight in sugar, but there is a fair amount of flesh-forming material present as well. Dates, without the stone, contain in 100 parts—

Water ..	20·8
Albumen	6·6
Sugar ..	54
Pectose and gum ..	12·3
Fat ..	0·2
Cellulose	5·5
Mineral matter ..	1·6

The pungent rigidity of the foliage protects the date from encroachment of pasture animals ; hence it can be left without fencing or hedging.

Queensland as a Date Country.

I have now given all the general information I can find in regard to the cultivation, &c., of the Date Palm in North Africa, Turkey in Asia, and Arabia. It will be convenient now to see if in Queensland similar conditions of temperature, &c., can be found. The part of Queensland which, bearing in mind the requirements of the plant already set forth, seems to be the most suitable for the cultivation of the *best* dates is to the west of Hughenden, Longreach, and Charleville, and from latitude 23deg. to the southern border of the colony. The following remarks all refer to this area :—

Temperature.

Comparing the region of Queensland which includes these places, with Biskra, in North Africa, in latitude 84deg. 51min. at an altitude of 410ft., we have

			Queensland.	Biskra
Annual average temperature ..	..	..	67·74	68·5
Mean temperature, coldest month	..	..	48·61	50·2
Mean temperature, hottest month	..	..	84·90	89·8

I do not know the extreme minimum temperature at Biskra, but the lowest in the part of Queensland above referred to is 26·4deg. at Boulia in July, 1894. My information for Queensland is obtained from the Meteorological Reports, which are only available from 1st September, 1893, to 31st August, 1894. I believe this last winter was considered a very cold one throughout the colony, and as the Date Palm can stand as low a temperature as 20deg. it should be safe even at Boulia from being killed by frost. The latitude 20deg. S. to 29deg. S. also indicates generally the area in which the suitable temperature is to be met with.

RAINFALL.—In the above possible date-growing belt of Queensland the rainfall ranges from 5in. to 24in., and in the more westerly portion this reaches the minor limit, therefore improving the quality of the date on account of the greater dryness of the air combined with the circumstance that there is greater heat also.

ALTITUDE.—Looking generally at West Queensland, the rivers and creeks all run to the south-west, showing that the higher ground is to the north and east. Then there are high downs between the Gulf of Carpentaria waters and the Diamantina and Thomson rivers; so that all this higher ground must vary from 600ft. to 1400ft. above sea level. But to the south-west of Boulia and Windorah, and to the south of Thargomindah and Charleville the altitude of the country is from sea level to 600ft. From the above figures it can easily be seen where there is the least likelihood of frost.

SOIL.—The geological formation in the region indicated is mesozoic, with desert sandstone on the higher ground between the various watersheds, and lower cretaceous on the plains and downs. As apparently the Date Palm prefers a sandy soil, the conditions in this case seem favourable also.

From the above data it will be seen that West Queensland is generally suited to the cultivation of the best dates. As to the local conditions, they must be ascertained by Queenslanders themselves; the object of this paper is to give to the colony the information in regard to the date which is scattered throughout many books and is not easily obtained, and also to suggest the best place for initiating experiments in date cultivation in this country.

CARDWELL BIRDS, WITH A FEW NOTES ON THOSE OF HERBERTON.

BY

KENDAL BROADBENT.

(Papers 1-VI read during 1892-4).

[This series being as yet incomplete its publication is delayed.-ED.]

AUSTRALIAN LEPIDOPTERA : THIRTY NEW SPECIES.

By *THOMAS P. LUCAS, M.R.C.S., Eng.*

L.S.A., LOND., L.R.C.P. & M., EDIN., &c.

(Read 15th November, 1894).

I HAVE again to thank Mr. Meyrick for his valued assistance, and also Messrs. Illidge and Relton for loan of specimens.

Group BOMBYCINA.
Family BOMBYCIDÆ.
BOMBYX PINNALIS, nov.sp.

♂ . 42 mm. Head wool-white Palpi iron-grey. Antennæ fuscous grey. Thorax wool-white, dorsal patch posteriorly iron-grey. Abdomen wool-white, with dorsum iron-grey continuous from thorax; caudal segment wool-white, narrowly bordered with black band. Forewings, costa straight; apex rounded, hindmargin rounded, wool-white, with ten to a dozen distinct or suffused sinuous undulating fuscous drab transverse lines, two of these border a wool-white line $\frac{2}{3}$ costa to $\frac{1}{3}$ inner margin ; two border a 2nd like line $\frac{3}{4}$ costa to $\frac{5}{8}$ inner margin ; a 3rd white line borders a conspicuous line of drab dots from $\frac{16}{16}$ costa to $\frac{16}{16}$ inner margin ; an indistinct smoke colour discoidal spot beyond half at $\frac{1}{3}$ from costa ; a smoky-black blotch on inner border $\frac{1}{6}$ to $\frac{1}{3}$; the wool shade prevails towards base and between 2nd and 3rd wool lines; the fuscous drab is suffused as a central transverse band, and apical and hindmarginal band. Cilia drab, based with grey. Hindwings wool-white, tinted with fuscous grey at base, crossed by a suffused fuscous-grey line $\frac{1}{2}$ costa to $\frac{4}{5}$ inner margin, and by a broad line of broken blotches (between veins), parallel with and $\frac{1}{6}$ from hindmargin. Cilia white, with fuscous grey base.

Two specimens at light ; Brisbane.

Bombyx fumosa, nov.sp.

♂. 35 mm. Head and antennæ red fuscous. Palpi smoky fuscous. Thorax fuscous black and fuscous red irrorated. Abdomen dark fuscous. Forewings, costa nearly straight; hindmargin rounded, coffee-fuscous with suffused irregular zig-zag transverse smoky fuscous lines over the whole wing; a discal red line at ¾ obliquely to median vein; costa smoky black, black suffused, hindmarginal line denticulate smoky fuscous. Cilia light fuscous grey. Hindwings ground colour as forewings, with fine scattered iron-grey scales. Cilia fuscous.

One specimen at light; Brisbane.

Bombyx Barnardi, nov.sp.

♂ ♀. 35-38 mm. Head and palpi creamy white. Antennæ-stalk white, pectinations black. Thorax creamy white, shoulders light fuscous, and gradually becoming fuscous posteriorly. Legs fuscous and ochreous annulated, with tufts of creamy ochreous on coxæ. Abdomen light fuscous, whiter in ♀. Forewings, costa straight, rounded at apex; hindmargin gently rounded, light fuscous with darker shadings towards base and costa, three wool-white transverse lines, 1st from ½ costa, sinuous and denticulate to within a fourth of inner margin, where it angles obliquely as a straight line to base of wing; 2nd from ⅔ costa, waved outward in first third, obliquely in second third, and inwards in inner third to ½ inner margin; 3rd a suffused line from near apex costa to ¾ inner margin, dotted with a series of dark fuscous spots and two curved lines; a white discal spot anteriorly to 2nd line, ⅓ from costa; in some instances 1st and 2nd lines joined nearer to inner border by a white line: in others 2nd white line is continued along costal margin to meet the 3rd line; submarginal line fuscous. Cilia light fuscous. Hindwings light fuscous, becoming darker toward base and along inner margin, submarginal line light fuscous. Cilia white, based with light fuscous.

Collected near Launceston, Tasmania, by the late George Barnard.

Bombyx ocularis, nov.sp.

♂. 22 mm. Head and palpi light iron-grey. Antennæ light fuscous. Thorax light fuscous, irrorated sparsely with grey and black, with a black dorsal line. Abdomen fuscous, irrorated with grey anteriorly, ochreous fuscous posteriorly. Forewings, costa straight, apex arched, hindmargin gently rounded, grey irrorated with fuscous and black, and marked with eye-like figures without the pupil, 1st close to base, in breadth to ½ inner margin, in depth to within ¼ costa, chocolate fuscous dusted with black and bordered interruptedly with black fuscous, and posteriorly by a white line ; 2nd figure on costal half, bounded anteriorly by chocolate band of cell, irregularly bordered with white, most conspicuously before apex, and crossed by chocolate-lined veins ; all veins chocolate-lined; submarginal and hindmarginal lines light fuscous. Cilia light fuscous, based with grey. Hindwings light fuscous, submarginal and marginal lines as forewings. Cilia as forewings.

One specimen ; Brisbane.

BOMBYX MURISOLENS, nov.sp.

♂ ♀. 32 mm. Head ochreous fuscous. Palpi fuscous-black. Antennæ-midrib deep fuscous, dentations lighter fuscous. Thorax and abdomen, mouse colour. Forewings, costa rounded, hindmargin gently rounded, mouse colour. Cilia dark fuscous. Hindwings as forewings, but not so thickly scaled.

The insect, when fresh caught, smells and scents the hand as a mouse.

Brisbane at light ; rare.

BOMBYX PICTA, nov.sp.

♂. 27 mm. Head black, face white, pinnæ black. Antennæ dark fuscous, pectinations dark iron-grey. Thorax blackish fuscous, shoulders tipped with white. Abdomen dark blackish fuscous, becoming black posteriorly. Forewings, costa slightly tortuous, hindmargin obliquely rounded, chocolate fuscous, thinly scaled, with hyaline dots and markings and black spots ; a row of rich velvety black spots from near base along costal border of median vein, with a round hyaline discal spot in middle, a line of black dots obliquely from basal spot of first line to inner margin before anal angle, a 3rd line of dots crossing this from ½ inner margin parallel with hindmargin to before apex, and continued along costa as far as discal spot; thus forming two irregular triangles of black spots; a white sinuous denticulate hyaline line from apex costa to $\frac{2}{3}$ inner margin, and there recurved to middle of second line, all black spots and line bordered with hyaline. Cilia chocolate fuscous with black dots at base. Hindwings chocolate'fuscous, more thickly scaled. Cilia as forewings.

One specimen at light ; Brisbane.

Family LIPARIDÆ.
DARALA RELTONI, nov.sp.

♂ . 52 mm. Head rich fuscous, face ferrous fuscous. Palpi ochreous fuscous. Antennæ midrib dark fuscous, pectinations narrowing at base and apex smoky fuscous. Legs fuscous, tibiæ alternately annulated with ochreous fuscous. Thorax deep fuscous. Abdomen fuscous, with ferruginous tint at base of segments. Forewings, costa gently rounded, hindmargin obliquely rounded, rich fuscous irrorated with shining silver-tipped fuscous scales and black scales, and giving the appearance of a tabby cat skin, *veins as channels, light ferrous with black linear borders*, a discal spot of ferrous bordered by a black ring beyond $\frac{1}{4}$ median subtending an indistinct fuscous line to $\frac{1}{2}$ inner margin, a darker smoky fuscous line parallel to hindmargin $\frac{4}{5}$ costa to $\frac{2}{3}$ inner margin. Cilia tabby-grey and fuscous. Hindwings as forewings.

Mr. Relton, Charleville.

ARTAXA COMPACTA, nov.sp.

♂ . 14 mm. Head, palpi and thorax ochreous fuscous. Antennæ fuscous, midrib darker fuscous. Abdomen ochreous fuscous, with a dorsal chocolate band broadening posteriorly. Forewings, costa rounded, apex rounded, hindmargin gently rounded, chocolate fuscous with a lunar fuscous ochreous patch having as base the middle $\frac{4}{6}$ of inner margin, and reaching to $\frac{1}{3}$ from costal margin, freely interspersed with fuscous scales ; an obscure ochreous dash at $\frac{3}{4}$ costa, banded by a dark-chocolate line anteriorly. Cilia chocolate. Hindwings dark-chocolate, with a triangle of fuscous ochreous in centre, apex at base of wing base $\frac{1}{3}$ from hindmargin. Cilia fuscous, fuscous ochreous on inner margin.

One specimen, Brisbane, at light.

Family NOTODONTIDÆ.

NOTODONTA NIGROLINEA, nov.sp.

♀. 50 mm.　Head iron-grey, face ochreous.　Palp ochreous fuscous.　Antennæ ochreous.　Thorax iron-grey.　Abdomen fuscous grey.　Forewings elongate, costa gently rounded, hindmargin rounded, iron-grey tinted with ochreous grey; three transverse rich velvety black lines, 1st almost straight from $\frac{1}{4}$ costa to $\frac{1}{6}$ inner margin; 2nd from $\frac{2}{5}$ costa, sinuous to $\frac{1}{3}$ inner margin; 3rd from $\frac{2}{3}$ costa, curved outward for one-third, thence nearly straight to $\frac{5}{6}$ inner margin; a dark suffusion between 1st and 2nd lines; a fuscous grey suffused band from $\frac{4}{5}$ costa to beyond median vein, denticulate on posterior border. Cilia iron grey.　Hindwings light fuscous grey, sparingly scattered with fuscous scales.　Cilia as forewings.

Brisbane.

Group NOCTUINA.

Family ORTHOSIIDÆ.

ORTHOSIA QUADRIPLANA, nov.sp.

♂ ♀. Head and antennæ fuscous grey. Palpi dark fuscous. Thorax anteriorly fuscous grey, collar edged with black, generally dark fuscous irrorated with black scales.　Abdomen dark iron-grey, bordered and transversely barred with fuscous. Forewings, costa straight, hindmargin gently rounded, fuscous grey, with a light purple tinge on basal third, a darker purple fuscous on middle third, and a more pronounced fuscous on posterior third, finely speckled and suffused with darker shades of fuscous and black, a velvety-black ? mark from costa at near base, suffused toward base before inner margin, a zig-zag scarcely traceable black line at $\frac{1}{4}$ costa lost in middle of wing; middle third of wing bordered anteriorly by a rich velvety slightly wavy black line, denticulate and finer toward inner margin, and posteriorly by a fine denticulate line from a rich black spot in costa, and enclosing a rich black kidney-shaped discal spot, opposite a triangular spot on costa; junction of middle and posterior thirds of a lighter purple over costal half; hindmarginal line ochreous fuscous.　Cilia dark fuscous.　Hindwings light fuscous, veins darker fuscous, hindmarginal line as forewings.　Cilia as forewings.

Brisbane, at light; rare.

Family HADENIDÆ.

HADENA DILUCESCEUS, nov.sp.

♂ ♀. 33-35 mm. Head, palpi, and thorax rich black. Antennæ midrib fuscous black, dentations dark fuscous. Abdomen bronzy fuscous with fine velvety black lines across segments, caudal appendage black. Forewings, costa straight, hindmargin gently rounded, bronzy black with lines and patches of rich velvety black; short velvety black lines along costa, an irregular angulated patch near base of cell, and a 2nd near centre of wing at $\frac{2}{5}$ across submedian ; outer divisions of veins velvety black. with a broad bar more or less suffused along posterior two-fifths of the wing at one-third distance from inner margin, a sinuous light fuscous hindmarginal line. Cilia black. Hindwings silvery-white, with a broad border of bronze black, narrow on inner margin ; hindmarginal line as forewings. Cilia bronze black.

Fernshaw and Moe, Victoria.

Family ANTHOPHILIDÆ.

THALPOCHARES FLAMMEOLA, nov.sp.

♂. 13 mm. Head, antennæ and palpi chocolate fuscous. Thorax reddish fuscous. Abdomen fuscous with fire colour bands at base of segments. Forewings, costa straight, hindmargin rounded, rich black fuscous tinted with fire colour, a fire colour band beyond middle, anterior border concaved for $\frac{1}{3}$, then angled obliquely to $\frac{1}{4}$ inner margin, posterior border convex to anterior and forming an irregular circle containing a darker shaded discal spot, thence parallel to anterior border at a line distance ; a kidney shape fire colour figure obliquely beyond hindmarginal half and almost diffused as one patch with it ; one or two irregular submarginal fire lines, and a fire patch near apex with a darker shading within. Cilia fuscous and fire coloured. Hindwings fiery red with a deep rich fuscous black hindmarginal border, narrowing to a point at anal angle. Cilia fuscous and fire colour.

Brisbane, at light.

THALPOCHARES IGNIFERA, nov.sp.

♂ ♀. 13-14 mm. Head and palpi fuscous flame colour. Antennæ fuscous. Thorax cinereous fuscous. Abdomen fuscous with yellow and flame colour at base of segments. Forewings,

costa straight, hindmargin rounded, rich chocolate fuscous tinged
with coppery red, and marked with dots, lines and shadings of
fuscous black, dark black fuscous spots on costa, a broad median
band with anterior and posterior dark border lines, anterior 4 or
5 dentate posteriorly, posterior costal half nearly straight,
bordered by a light yellow line, forming a spot on costa, thence
broadly angled toward apex and enclosing a yellow square spot,
thence obliquely, once dentate to before $\frac{3}{4}$ inner margin ; posterior third of wing more fiery tinted, and crossed by one or two
darker or lighter lines. Cilia yellow and fuscous. Hindwings red
fire colour, with a dark fuscous hindborder narrowing before
anal angle. Cilia deep fuscous.

Brisbane, at light.

THALPOCHARES PECTORORA, nov.sp.

♂ ♀ . 15-18 mm. Head and palpi light chocolate fuscous.
Antennæ cinereous fuscous. Thorax cinereous fuscous, tinted
with light lavender. Abdomen reddish fuscous. Forewings,
costa waved, apex acutely angled, hindmargin angled at vein 4,
light cinereous fuscous, tinted with lavender colour and marked
with lines and bands of rufous fuscous, a red-brown dot at $\frac{1}{4}$
costa, a 2nd at $\frac{1}{2}$ obliquely elongated, a like one at $\frac{3}{4}$, and sub-
apical and apical dots : a broad rufous fuscous band or shield
across wing, with deep ferrous anterior border lines from $\frac{3}{4}$ costa
obliquely and anteriorly to median, and containing an ill-defined
discal spot, thence to $\frac{1}{4}$ inner margin ; posterior border, irregularly parallel and near to hindmargin, frequently dentate, with
a border of light lavender : hindmarginal line light lavender.
Cilia reddish fuscous. Hindwings light cinereous lavender, with
the broad central continuation of the shield of forewings, with
4 or 5 transverse ferrous fuscous lines, posterior denticulate and
roughly parallel with hindmargin : hindmarginal and cilia as
forewings.

Brisbane.

THALPOCHARES PLUTONIS, nov.sp.

♂ ♀ . 14-18 mm. Head, palpi, antennæ, and thorax rufous
ferrous. Abdomen ochreous ferrous, darker posteriorly. Forewings, costa rounded, hindmargin obliquely rounded, rufous
ferrous, tinted with darker shadings and marked with yellow
spots of fire colour at $\frac{1}{4}$, $\frac{3}{4}$ and along apex of costa, a small yellow

dot in centre of wing at $\frac{2}{3}$, hindmarginal yellow line. Cilia rufous fuscous. Hindwings as forewings in colour, with an indistinct diffused darker median line; hindmarginal line and cilia as forewings.

Mr. Pilcher, Rockhampton.

THALPOCHARES CONCINNA, nov.sp.

♂ ♀. 12-14 mm. Head, palpi, antennæ, thorax, and abdomen light ochreous cinereous. Forewings, costa straight, hindmargin gently rounded, light ochreous cinereous, sparingly and irregularly shaded with darker shadings, obscure white dots on apical third of costa, a darker fuscous discal spot at $\frac{2}{3}$ near costa; in some shaded, in others with a darker border line; an inconspicuous denticulate sinuous dark line bordered posteriorly with ochreous line from $\frac{4}{5}$ costa to $\frac{2}{3}$ inner margin; submarginal light and darker denticulate lines. Cilia as wings. Hindwings as forewings, with an inconspicuous darker transverse denticulate line at $\frac{7}{8}$ in a few specimens. Cilia as forewing.

Brisbane; among grass.

Family EUCLIDIDÆ.

FODINA INFRACTAFINIS, nov.sp.

♀. 45 mm. Head, palpi, and thorax ochreous brick-red. Antennæ slate colour, ochreous tinted at base. Abdomen smoky fuscous. Forewings, costa nearly straight. Apex acute, hindmargin gently rounded, smoky fuscous with a decided chocolate tinge, a triangle of diffused white spots at base, two touching costa, a small diffused white spot at $\frac{1}{4}$ costa, a broad white band $\frac{1}{3}$-$\frac{1}{2}$ costa extending to $\frac{1}{5}$-$\frac{1}{2}$ inner margin, a white patch at $\frac{3}{4}$ costa, hindmarginal band and cilia white. Hindwings smoky fuscous, hindmarginal band white smoky at apical and anal angles. Cilia as hindmarginal band.

Throughout Northern Queensland.

Allied to *F. Schroderi*, Feld., but colour of fore wings fuscous and not black, straight-cut median white band, and straight-banded border, readily distinguish it from that species.

Family THERMESIIADÆ.

THERMESIA CARIOSA, nov.sp.

♂ ♀. 17-18 mm. Head, antennæ, thorax, and abdomen light ochreous. Palpi ochreous fuscous. Forewings, costa gently rounded, hindmargin obliquely rounded, creamy ochreous

with five transverse light ferrous-drab lines like worm trails,
1st from $\frac{1}{6}$ inner margin quickly fades into ground colour, 2nd
$\frac{1}{3}$ inner border to median vein, thence diffused in ground colour,
3rd from $\frac{3}{4}$ inner border to centre of wing, thence obliquely outwards for a short distance straight and then obliquely inward to
$\frac{3}{5}$ costa, 4th more diffused from $\frac{7}{8}$ inner margin, where it is often
divided into two lines, to opposite costal angle of third line,
5th submarginal, a black dot at $\frac{1}{3}$ costa, a line of 3 black dots $\frac{1}{2}$
costa to median vein, two black dots beyond $\frac{3}{4}$ costa, a hindmarginal row darker in costal half.   Cilia light fuscous, with a
narrow ochreous line.   Hindwings as forewings, with four worm-
like tracings with a small black dot between 1st and 2nd, hindmarginal row of black dots faint.   Cilia as forewings.

Brisbane at light ; rare.

Family HYPÆNIDÆ.

HYPÆNA UMBRIFERA, nov.sp.

♂ ♀ . 18-20 mm.   Head and antennæ light cinereous fuscous.   Palpi fuscous.   Thorax and abdomen fuscous shot with
light purplish shade.   Forewings, costa straight, apex acute,
hindmargin rounded, light cinereous fuscous, more or less
variable in different specimens, shaded with darker fuscous, veins
darker fuscous, in some posteriorly as fuscous bars ; two wavy,
denticulate dark fuscous lines more or less parallel with hind-
margin, 1st $\frac{1}{4}$ costa to $\frac{1}{3}$ inner margin, 2nd $\frac{3}{4}$ costa to $\frac{2}{3}$ inner
margin ; between these is a median band of dark fuscous,
suffused and less distinct toward costa, and in some specimens a
kidney shape discal spot nearer costa, a row of light ochreous
dots across wing at $\frac{7}{8}$ in some specimens obscured with fuscous,
hindmarginal fine fuscous and ochreous lines alternately.   Cilia
fuscous based with ochreous.   Hindwings light cinereous fuscous, with shaded discal fuscous spot before middle, a circular
line $\frac{3}{5}$ costa to $\frac{1}{2}$ inner margin, a parallel broad band at $\frac{4}{5}$ divided
by an ochreous line into two ; a submarginal line of lunulate
loops, hindmarginal lines as forewings.   Cilia ochreous tinted
with fuscous.

Brisbane ; in bogs and wet grassy places.

HYPÆNA CHALCIAS, m.ss. Meyr.

♂ ♀ . 20-25 mm.   Head lavender-grey.   Palpi and antennæ cinereous fuscous.   Thorax lavender-grey.   Abdomen

fuscous drab with reddish fuscous at base of segments. Forewings, costa straight, apex very acute, hindmargin rounded,
light whitish lavender suffused with grey toward costa, and as a
band on inner border, a dark fuscous triangular patch from base
along median to $\frac{1}{2}$ ending in a darker spot with a black dot half
way to costa, a rich fuscous colour line $\frac{2}{3}$ costa obliquely half-
way to hind border, then angled on itself obliquely to $\frac{1}{2}$ inner
margin ; behind this latter part is a broad suffused fuscous patch,
near hindmargin, banding a staircase of yellow or bronze-tinted
steps broadest at hindmargin, narrowing to a point opposite $\frac{1}{2}$
hindmargin ; hindmarginal line dark fuscous. Cilia lavender-
grey base with whitish lavender. Hindwings fuscous, veins
darker fuscous. Cilia fuscous varied with cinereous fuscous.

Brisbane ; rare.

HYPÆNA INNOCUA, nov.sp.

♀ . 25 mm. Head and antennæ light grey. Palpi fuscous.
Thorax light grey, inclining to ochreous fuscous posteriorly.
Abdomen ochreous fuscous. Forewings, costa straight, apical
third rounded, apex acute, hindmargin sinuous, rounded, light
ochreous fuscous, with darker fuscous scales on veins and crossed
by three sinuous denticulate outward bowed fuscous lines, the
innermost banded anteriorly and the two outer ones banded
posteriorly with an ochreous line, 1st line from $\frac{2}{3}$ costa to $\frac{1}{4}$ inner
margin, thrice dentate anteriorly : 2nd line from $\frac{4}{5}$ costa to $\frac{2}{3}$
inner margin, thrice dentate anteriorly. inner dentation denticu-
late : 3rd line from $\frac{4}{5}$ costa to $\frac{3}{4}$ inner margin. dentations
parallel with 2nd line, a short indistinct fuscous bar opposite
1st dentation of 2nd line, a fine ochreous fuscous hindmarginal
line. Cilia fuscous. Hindwings as forewings, 1st line wanting;
2nd line $\frac{3}{4}$ costa to $\frac{1}{4}$ inner margin, darker on inner $\frac{2}{3}$; 3rd line
$\frac{4}{5}$ costa to anal angle of hindmargin. Cilia as forewings.

Brisbane ; rare.

HYPÆNA SIMPLEX, nov.sp.

♂ ♀ . 16 mm. Head, palpi, antennæ, thorax, and abdomen
a soft fawn colour fuscous. Forewings, costa straight, apex
acute, hindmargin gently rounded, fawn colour fuscous, indistinctly irregularly shaded with darker scales, and pepper-like
dusting ; a black discal spot beyond $\frac{1}{2}$ subtends a darker diffused
band to $\frac{2}{3}$ inner margin, a darker suffusion on hindmargin, a

double fine hindmarginal black line. Cilia light fawn tipped with darker fuscous. Hindwings as forewings, with a discal black dot before $\frac{1}{2}$ and two indistinct light transverse lines at $\frac{2}{3}$ and $\frac{3}{4}$, hindmarginal double line, and cilia as forewings.

Geraldton and North Queensland.

Allied to *H. umbrifera*, Lucas, but lighter forewings with fewer markings, and darker, suffused grey, hindwings.

HYPŒNA (?) MULTITRICHA, nov.sp.

♂ ♀ . 26-28 mm. Head and antennæ light ochreous fuscous. Palpi ochreous, very hairy, terminal joint a light fuscous brush of hairs. Thorax ochreous fuscous tinted with darker fuscous. Abdomen ochreous. Forewings, costa slightly wavy, apex angled, hindmargin sinuous, roundly angled at vein 4, light ochreous, freely speckled, with dots and dashes of chocolate fuscous ; an interrupted irregular band from $\frac{1}{3}$ inner margin to just short of $\frac{1}{2}$ costa where it is diffused round a yellow lined dumb-bell-shaped discal spot ; a rich chocolate fuscous zigzag line $\frac{3}{4}$ costa to submedian bordered posteriorly by a line of ground colour and a suffused patch of fuscous extending to apex ; a hind-marginal row of small chocolate fuscous dots. Cilia ochreous. Hindwings as forewings freely covered with single fuscous scales, and four more or less well-marked transverse sinuous denticulate red fuscous lines, hindmarginal irregular row of dots ; cilia as forewings.

Moe and Fernshaw, Victoria. One specimen, Brisbane.

HYPŒNA (?) PRÆSTANS, nov.sp.

♀ . 28 mm. Head violet fuscous. Palpi fuscous, terminal joint a brush of brown hairs. Antennæ ochreous drab, pecti-nations fuscous. Thorax violet fuscous with black-tipped hairs. Abdomen light-drab fuscous. Forewings, costa gently rounded, apex acute, hindborder concave between apex and vein 4, extended at vein 4, thence obliquely straight to anal angle, violet fuscous, with black-scaled and lighter and darker shadings, a darker-chocolate fuscous suffusion at base, a median transverse band of the same, with darker bounding lines and dots, three or four small reddish ochreous dots in black ring on median and submedian in centre third, a circuitous line of black dots beyond median band, a row of three deep chocolate fuscous spots with a dividing line of ochreous, subtended from costa before apex,

I

five or six dots of black along costa, hindmarginal line of black dots. Cilia violet fuscous. Hindwings ochreous drab, suffused with smoky-grey, and banded by three transverse dentate black lines, hindmarginal line of black dots. Cilia ochreous drab with patches of smoky fuscous.

One specimen at light, Brisbane.

HYPŒNA TRANSITA, nov.sp.

♂ ♀. 18-20 mm. Head and antennæ light-chocolate fuscous. Palpi light fuscous, terminal joint hair-like and plumed, re-curved. Thorax light purplish-chocolate with fuscous dots. Abdomen light fuscous, with darker dorsal dots on 1st and 2nd segments, with diffused fuscous rings on hind segments. Forewings, costa nearly straight, apex acute, hindmargin bowed in middle, light-chocolate purplish fuscous, with darker fuscous shadings and black lines and markings. A dark fuscous dot near base close to costa, a wavy linear dark fuscous line from ⅓ costa to ⅕ inner margin, preceded by suffused lines of black and dark fuscous forming an irregular median band, a seahorse-shaped figure from opposite ¾ costa to ⅔ inner margin, black and mixed fuscous, a dark suffused line from costal angle to hindmargin just before apex, hindmarginal line of circular dots. Cilia fuscous. Hindwings light-purplish fuscous, with indistinct median line and a fine dark hindmarginal line. Cilia as forewings.

Geraldton and North Queensland generally. Allied to H. læsalis, Walk.

Family HERMINIIADÆ.

HERMINIA ASSERTA, nov.sp.

♂ ♀. 20 mm. Head, palpi, antennæ and thorax fuscous drab. Abdomen fuscous drab. Forewings, costa straight, hindmargin rounded, fuscous drab, irrorated with ochreous fuscous, veins darker fuscous, a deep-black conspicuous discal spot beyond half ⅓ from costa, a crenulate indistinct watermark and fuscous ochreous line ¾ costa to ⅔ inner margin, a 2nd like line from just before apex of costa to ⅝ hindmargin, a fine hindmarginal and two submarginal fuscous lines alternating with fuscous ochreous lines or dots. Cilia fuscous barred with ochreous fuscous. Hindwings creamy ochreous sparingly irrorated with fuscous grey, veins fuscous, an interrupted indistinct crenulate fuscous line beyond $\frac{3}{4}$ costa to $\frac{1}{2}$ inner margin, a 2nd and 3rd darker and more distinct at $\frac{3}{4}$ to $\frac{5}{6}$ costa to anal angle ; hind-marginal and submarginal lines as forewings.   Cilia as fore-wings.

Brisbane.

MADOPA CURVATA, nov.sp.

♂ ♀ . 17-21 mm. Head light and violet grey, face whiter. Palpi grey.   Antennæ light fuscous.   Thorax fuscous grey, tinted with violet.   Abdomen light fuscous grey.   Forewings, costa nearly straight, hindmargin rounded at vein 4, light grey; others light fuscous, tinted with violet ; a black spot on costa $\frac{1}{12}$, subtending a smaller one and less distinct, a conspicuous black patch at $\frac{1}{4}$ costa, prolonged as a sinuous line to $\frac{1}{3}$ inner margin, shaded near costa with obscure shading and a small four-angled discal spot ; a black band beyond $\frac{1}{2}$ costa, arched broadly outwards to enclose an elongated discoidal spot ; thence obliquely inwards to $\frac{1}{2}$ inner margin ; an irregular shading of spots near and parallel with hindmargin in some specimens ; hindmarginal row of black dots. Cilia as wings. Hindwings as forewings with an indistinct patch of shading at $\frac{2}{3}$ near costa, a black line at $\frac{1}{3}$ inner margin parallel with hindmargin and gradually becoming lighter toward costa where it is hardly discernible ; another like and parallel line beyond anal angle, but more rapidly becoming lighter shade ; hindmarginal row of short lines. Cilia as wings.

Rockhampton ; Mr. Pilcher.

MADOPA LIGATA, nov.sp.

♂ . 18 mm. Head, palpi, antennæ and thorax light choco-late fuscous. Abdomen light fuscous. Forewings, costa nearly straight, hindmargin waved, rounded, light violet fuscous, costa reddish ochreous, a small black discal spot at $\frac{2}{3}$, a black curved attenuated line from costa just before apex obliquely to median vein, hindmarginal band reddish ochreous.   Cilia ochreous fus-cous. Hindwings fuscous tinted with ochreous and bordered with a suffused darker border. Cilia as forewings.

One specimen ; Brisbane.

MADOPA AURICULARIA, nov.sp.

♂ ♀ . 19-20 mm.   Head and thorax purplish fuscous. Palpi chocolate fuscous.   Antennæ light fuscous.   Abdomen light purplish fuscous. Forewings costa straight, hindmargin gently rounded, purple fuscous, more or less tinted with violet or redish ochreous ; the whole wing is indistinctly marbled by transverse ochreous fuscous lines and spots ; six or seven sharp-angled black dots along costa from $\frac{1}{6}$ to before apex ; an oblique line of dots transversely at $\frac{1}{6}$, a broad auricular figure of suffused black and dark fuscous $\frac{1}{2}$ to $\frac{3}{4}$ costa and curving round to a line of interrupted dots to $\frac{3}{4}$ costa, enclosed space light ochreous or purple fuscous, a curved sinuous double ochreous black line from costa immediately beyond to $\frac{4}{5}$ inner margin, an indistinct submarginal fuscous line, a hindmarginal line of black dots. Cilia as ground colour. Hindwings ochreous fuscous or light violet fuscous, irrorated with darker scales, hindmarginal line of black. Cilia as forewings.

Rockhampton and Brisbane.

Group TINEINA.
Family XYLORICTIDÆ.
LICHENAULA OXYGONA, nov.sp.

♀. 26 mm. Head creamy-white. Palpi creamy-white, terminal joint smoky-grey. Antennæ golden-cream. Thorax creamy-white, shading into grey posteriorly. Abdomen creamy fuscous. Forewings elongate, costa gently rounded, hindmargin nearly straight, rich creamy-white finely irrorated with smoky-grey scales ; costal line ochreous, beyond costal band of ground-colour from base narrowing at $\frac{1}{2}$ costa, and extending in a narrow line to $\frac{1}{4}$ inner margin ; a fuscous line $\frac{1}{4}$ costa obliquely shading into grey to median to within one-sixth of hindmargin, thence angled in a recurved outward line to before anal angle of inner margin ; this line is bordered posteriorly by a line of ground-colour which runs along veins shaded with grey to hindmargin, these form alternate lines with grey suffused bands ; three choco-late fuscous spots beyond on costa, the third giving off two lines, the first bordered posteriorly with white runs nearly parallel with hindmargin to just before anal angle of inner margin ; the second, which is parallel, stops short at $\frac{1}{3}$ hindmargin. Cilia grey. Hindwings cream-colour, shaded, excepting all borders, with smoky-grey ; short marginal fuscous band round apex to $\frac{1}{6}$ hind-margin. Cilia white, grey toward apex.

One specimen bred from the caterpillar taken in scrub near Brisbane by Mr. Illidge, 1893.

INDEX.

(Authors and Subjects).

www.ingramcontent.com/pod-product-compliance
Lightning Source LLC
Chambersburg PA
CBHW030625270326
41927CB00007B/1309